VEGETARIAN FOOD FOR *healthy kids*

NICOLA GRAIMES

NOURISH

EAT WELL, LIVE WELL

Vegetarian Food for Healthy Kids
Nicola Graimes

First published in the UK and USA in 2016 by Nourish,
an imprint of Watkins Media Limited
19 Cecil Court
London WC2N 4EZ

enquiries@nourishbooks.com

Publisher: Jo Lal
Managing Editor: Rebecca Woods
Editor: Wendy Hobson
Managing Designer: Viki Ottewill
Designer: Allan Sommerville
Illustrations: Allan Sommerville
Commissioned photography: Tony Briscoe
Food Stylist: Rebecca Woods
Prop Stylist: Lucy Harvey
Production: Uzma Taj

A CIP record for this book is available from the British Library

ISBN: 978-1-84899-306-8

10 9 8 7 6 5 4 3 2 1

Typeset in Lino Letter and Goodlife
Colour reproduction by XY Digital
Printed in China

Notes on the Recipes
Unless otherwise stated:
– Use medium eggs, fruit and vegetables
– Use fresh ingredients, including herbs and spices
– Do not mix metric and imperial measurements
– 1 tsp = 5ml   1 tbsp = 15ml   1 cup = 240ml

Publisher's Note
While every care has been taken in compiling the recipes for
this book, Watkins Media Limited, or any other persons who
have been involved in working on this publication, cannot accept
responsibility for any errors or omissions, inadvertent or not,
that may be found in the recipes or text, nor for any problems
that may arise as a result of preparing one of these recipes.
If you are pregnant or breastfeeding or have any special dietary
requirements or medical conditions, it is advisable to consult
a medical professional before following any of the recipes
contained in this book.

nourishbooks.com

CONTENTS

HELLO

Every parent wants the best for their children and top of the list for most of us is good health. The theory is so simple: just eat nutritious foods, drink enough water and cut out the junk. But we know that's light years away from what happens in practice. There's children's fickle eating habits and tastes to take into account, peer pressure, time constraints and so many other things that make it much more difficult to keep them (let alone ourselves) on the right track.

I don't profess to be the perfect role model, but experience has taught me a lot about helping my children to make the right dietary choices, from offering a varied and interesting range of meals and snacks to engaging them in food shopping and cooking (and at times growing) their own foods. So I was reassured recently to read a health report that said those children who help out in the kitchen and have a basic knowledge of nutrition are more likely to be on the right path for eating healthily as adults – and that makes a lot of sense as it inspires an interest in food and a greater willingness to try different things.

Yet I'm also a realist. Research shows that pizza, pasta, burgers, sausages and curry remain

MEAL PLANNING

To make meal planning and preparation easier and more convenient, some recipes come with handy symbols. These highlight whether the recipe (or its main constituent) is suitable for freezing, making ahead or in bulk.

Suitable for freezing

Make ahead

 Make in bulk

all-time favourite meals with children, veggie or not. No big surprises there, but I've been eager in this book to give you healthier versions of these popular foods. For instance, against all odds, pizza with a base made from grated cauliflower mixed with ground almonds goes down really well at home (see page 128), while who'd have thought a mixture of pumpkin seeds, chestnuts and Cheddar cheese could be transformed into great-tasting, nutritious sausages (see page 134)?

These ideas and many more can be found within the pages of *Vegetarian Food for Healthy Kids*. There are recipes for all times of the day and week, from sustaining Breakfasts and energizing Lunches to refuelling After-School Snacks and nourishing Weekday Meals to health-giving suggestions for the Weekend. And you'll also find recipes for the occasional fruity sweet treat, with a keen eye, on my part, on keeping the sugar content to a minimum.

Time is at a premium for us all, so I've added Quick Ideas within each chapter to give you healthy, pocket-size suggestions for bumping-up the nutritional value of a meal. And for me, one of the most important and exciting features in the book is the Kids Cook (see below) pages, including a collection of easy, nutritious recipes for children to make – perhaps with you at their side as kitchen assistant.

KIDS COOK

Learning to cook is such a vital life skill. Encouraging your children to join you in the kitchen is one of the most useful and enjoyable ways of helping them to be more food knowledgeable and health aware. What's more, most children love cooking – and for parents it gets them away from screens!

That's why in this book I've included the Kids Cook features, which give a collection of recipes for children to make on their own or with the help of an adult, depending on their level of experience. They'll have fun making everything from simple fruit- and veg-filled smoothies and tasty, healthy sandwich fillings to the slightly more challenging but no less delicious Sunday lunch.

IN A NUTSHELL

What we eat – and our lifestyles – directly affects how we feel and our health. The same goes for our children. In essence, for me it all boils down to these three things:

1 DUMP THE JUNK
Say goodbye to sugary processed foods and drinks. The same goes for hydrogenated fats and additives.

2 DRINK WATER
Good hydration is vital for both mental and physical health.

3 GET ACTIVE
Exercise helps us maintain a healthy weight as well as boosting memory and concentration.

GET HEALTHY ACTION PLAN

Many studies highlight the numerous positive health benefits of a vegetarian diet. However, cutting out meat is only part of the picture . . . a veggie diet is only healthy if it is varied and balanced. A diet of processed veggie burgers or pizza, fizzy drinks and confectionery may be meat-free, but it's also low in nutritional value. So what should a healthy vegetarian child be eating? The following are top of my list:

1. KICK-START THE DAY

The research is all there. Children who eat a nutritious, varied breakfast perform better at school and are more alert and focused. Health experts seem to agree the first meal of the day is also the most important as it kick-starts the metabolism, replenishing vital brain nutrients and blood-sugar levels that have diminished overnight.

Skipping breakfast makes kids grouchy and can lead to a habit of snacking on unhealthy foods, such as the grabbed packet of crisps/potato chips on the way to school or a sugared doughnut mid-morning.

I'm a bit of a stickler when it comes to breakfast. It may take a little extra time to prepare, but a nutritious breakfast is the best start you can give your children and it could make all the difference to their mental and physical wellbeing. Ideally, breakfast should be a combination of energizing wholegrain starches, satisfying protein, fresh fruit or veg and healthy fats. For inspiration turn to pages 12–35, or the quick, tasty ideas below.

BREAKFAST BOOSTERS

⇨ Wholegrain toast with Miso Butter (see page 23), topped with a poached egg and served with a glass of diluted fresh fruit juice.

⇨ Chia seeds soaked in nut milk with fresh or dried fruit, nuts, seeds, oats and ground linseeds/flaxseeds.

⇨ Low sugar and salt baked beans on wholegrain toast with an egg or chopped avocado and a sprinkling of nutritional yeast flakes, served with a glass of diluted fresh fruit juice.

⇨ Toasted wholegrain bread rolls with soft cheese, chopped banana and toasted sunflower seeds. Or try grilled/broiled tomatoes or mushrooms instead of the banana.

⇨ No-added sugar, wholegrain breakfast cereal with nut milk, fresh fruit and ground linseeds/flaxseeds and chopped nuts.

⇨ Fruit smoothies with ground hemp seeds and a spoonful of peanut butter. Or try a mixture of fruit with vegetables.

2. SNACK ATTACK

If your children are anything like mine, then food is never far from their minds. And with good reason: the young have high energy requirements relative to their size and in general need two to three nutritious, energy-dense snacks to fill the gaps between main meals. Ditch nutrient-deficient sugary or high-fat snacks in favour of those with a combination of protein, wholegrain starches and beneficial omega fats to keep blood-sugar levels stable and ensure sustained energy through to mealtime. Here are a few simple ideas but you'll discover plenty more snack ideas on pages 62–81.

SNACKTASTIC

⇨ Red pepper houmous (see page 46) with wholegrain rice cakes or rye crackers and carrot sticks.

⇨ Vegetable or bean pâté on Seeded Oatcakes (see page 66) with a sprinkling of nutritional yeast flakes.

⇨ Omelette filled with cheese, pesto, diced tomato and finely chopped fresh spinach.

⇨ Wholegrain pitta bread filled with grated cheese, apple or pear and chopped walnuts.

⇨ Peanut butter and grated egg on toasted wholegrain bread rolls.

⇨ Quesadillas filled with tomato pesto, mozzarella and rocket/arugula.

⇨ Hard-boiled eggs dunked into Spicy-Nutty Savoury Crunch (see page 69).

3. EAT UP YOUR GREENS . . . AND YOUR YELLOW, RED . . .

Probably the biggest challenge for most parents is to get their children to eat vegetables, and to enjoy a variety of fresh produce in particular. Health experts recommend children eat at least three portions of different veg and two of fruit a day, so that can be a single fruit such as an apple or pear, or the amount that will fit into one hand of, say, peas or broccoli florets, or a glass of fresh fruit juice (best diluted with water). A helping of canned beans or pulses/legumes also counts towards the five-a-day. It's an ongoing challenge for most parents, but hopefully the following tips may help to inspire.

FRESH VEGGIE IDEAS

⇨ Young children find brassicas bitter in flavour, so an inherent dislike of cabbage, sprouts, broccoli and cauliflower from an early age is hardly surprising. Try taming any bitterness by combining brassicas with a dairy element, such as a cheese or a creamy, nutty sauce, or by adding spices.

⇨ Add finely chopped or grated vegetables to familiar popular dishes such as pizza, pasta sauces, lasagne, soups, stews and curries.

▷ Eat a rainbow: different-coloured fruit and vegetables provide a range of health properties. Why not try creating a game of identifying and sampling fruit and vegetables of various hues?

▷ Present fruit and vegetables in different ways – raw vegetables often go down better than cooked varieties, and they're also good for dunking and eating with the hands rather than cutlery, which is always a winner.

▷ Be inventive in the way you cook fresh produce: roasted, chargrilled, stir-fried and baked are sometimes more accepted than simply boiled or steamed.

▷ Subterfuge is always an option and you'll find sneaky suggestions throughout the book, from adding vegetables to fruit smoothies (see page 32) or to a filling for Chinese Potstickers (see page 116), or pimping-up the nutritional value of sauces by adding puréed vegetables or pulses/legumes (see page 100).

4. MAIN IDEAS

I try to keep a mental list of the meals we'll be eating at home over the week ahead. This not only makes food shopping easier to plan, but also ensures we're all eating a good variety of foods. It's all too easy to get stuck in a rut but I find this works for me (along with the ideas on the right) and is a perfect way of keeping meals fresh and varied.

MEALS WITH THE X-FACTOR

▷ Spice it up! Forget bland – research has found that most kids love stronger flavours, such as meals livened up with spices. In the book, you'll find spiced-up dishes such as Cheesy-Peas Cashew Korma (page 110) and Big Veg Chilli (page 120).

▷ Similarly, an intriguing piece of research by Japanese nutritionists found that children love foods with umami flavours – that satisfying savoury taste found in foods such as soy sauce or Parmesan cheese. Use this to your advantage by stir-frying veg with a splash of low-salt soy sauce or adding a sprinkling of Parmesan to vegetable fritters (see page 61).

▷ Carbs may have fallen out of favour in recent times, but they remain an essential source of energy for children. Choose slow-release starchy foods such as quinoa, brown rice, sweet potatoes and wholegrain bread.

▷ When it comes to protein, variety is key. To get a full spectrum of amino acids – the building blocks of protein – try to give your children a good range of proteins from different sources such as eggs, dairy products, nuts, beans, lentils, tofu and other soy foods.

▷ Some of our most successful family meals have an element of fun. This can be as simple as laying everything out on the table and letting everyone help themselves – or as I call them 'assembly meals' – such as the Build-Your-Own Tacos (see page 138).

Likewise, getting kids to help out with the cooking can be both educational and enjoyable – famous last words!

WHAT DO VEGGIE KIDS NEED?

A varied, balanced vegetarian diet can provide all the nutrients your child needs, but it's advisable to be aware that the following nutrients are not as richly available in a meat-free diet as they are in one that contains animal produce or fish.

IRON

Iron deficiency is extremely common and not just among vegetarians. Iron is essential for healthy oxygenated red blood cells and a lack of the mineral may show itself as tiredness, irritability, poor concentration and development.

It's worth noting that iron from animal sources is more readily absorbed by the body than that found in eggs and plant foods. That said, eating or drinking something rich in vitamin C, such as a glass of fresh orange juice, or fruit and vegetables, at the same time as eating a vegetarian iron-rich meal will certainly help boost absorption of the mineral.

Good veggie sources: eggs, beans, lentils, nuts, seeds, oats, fortified breakfast cereals and bread, molasses, nutritional yeast flakes, green leafy vegetables and dried fruit.

OMEGA-3 FATS

Much has been reported of the health benefits of omega-3 fatty acids on the brain, skin, joints and heart. The active components DHA, EPA and GLA can be found in certain vegetarian foods, especially the examples below, although those found in fish oils are more potent. It is for this reason that some dieticians recommend vegetarians take an omega-3 supplement daily.

Good veggie sources: walnuts, hemp seeds, chia seeds, linseeds/flaxseeds, rapeseeds/canola seeds, green leafy vegetables and fortified eggs and milk.

VITAMIN B$_{12}$

Important for healthy blood, growth and brain function as well as energy metabolism – so essential for children and adults – this vitamin is found in beneficial amounts in animal products, but you can also find it in plant-based foods, albeit in smaller quantities.

Good veggie sources: dairy products, eggs, yeast, yeast extract, fortified breakfast cereals and bread, tofu and soy products.

SUGAR AND SPICE . . .

In our house, sweet treats are not completely off limits. I may be castigated for this but I think moderation is key. If you remove something utterly and completely, it can lead to bingeing if the opportunity arises, so I reckon a little bit of what you fancy does little harm. It's also more realistic when you factor in that children have a naturally sweet tooth.

So that means you will find some desserts and sweet treats in this book, but added refined sugar is kept to a minimum. I prefer to use honey, maple syrup and blackstrap molasses, and, while I'm fully aware that these are sugar by another name, each one provides some nutritional value. For instance, good-quality unfiltered honey is antibacterial, while maple syrup has antioxidant properties, and blackstrap molasses provides iron, calcium, potassium, magnesium, selenium and B$_6$.

GOING LOW-SUGAR

The World Health Organization recently recommended that the amount of added sugar a child eats is halved to less than 6 teaspoons per day. The following tips may help you to cut the sweet stuff.

▷ I'm a big fan of using spices, including cinnamon, nutmeg, ginger and mixed/apple pie spice, instead of sugar as a natural sweetener. Pure vanilla extract is also useful for adding a touch of sweetness – though bear in mind some brands do contain added sugar.

▷ As with salt, it's possible to gradually curb a taste for sweet things. Start by avoiding sprinkling sugar over breakfast cereals as well as slightly tart fruit such as strawberries, raspberries and grapefruit, and the same goes for pancakes and fruit smoothies.

▷ Swap shop-bought fruit yogurts with plain yogurt and stir in homemade fruit purées or chopped fruit.

▷ A square of good-quality dark/bittersweet chocolate has less added sugar than milk or white chocolate and can be just as much of a treat.

CHEERS TO WATER!

Most children don't drink enough water, or fluids in general, and thirst can often be confused for hunger. Proper hydration is as important for concentration, mental clarity and energy as a good diet. Just consider that a 2 per cent loss in body fluids can lead to a staggering 20 per cent reduction in physical and mental performance.

Soft fizzy drinks are some of the biggest offenders for added sugar, but shop-bought smoothies, fruit drinks, energy drinks and even some flavoured waters can all be sugar-laden too. The presence of caffeine will increase dehydration and play havoc with sleep patterns.

GOOD DRINKING TIPS

The recommended amount for school-age children is around 6 glasses of fluids a day and here are a few suggestions for those to opt for.

▷ Water is best – tapped, bottled, still or carbonated (try flavouring it yourself with slices of orange, lemon, cucumber, berries or mint).

▷ Freshly squeezed fruit juices (dilute half and half with water).

⇨ Fruit and herb teas.

⇨ Unsweetened coconut water.

⇨ Unsweetened nut and coconut milk.

⇨ Milk – cows', goats', sheep's or dairy-free.

⇨ Homemade smoothies – a great way of boosting fruit intake as well as sneaking in some veg (see pages 32–35).

THE POWER OF EXERCISE

Exercise is just as important as good diet when it comes to health. A recent study shockingly revealed that up to 69 per cent of children are largely inactive – yet physical activity is fundamentally important for a healthy body as well as an active mind, benefiting concentration, memory and focus.

TIME TO GET ACTIVE . . .

Bear in mind that school-age children require about an hour of aerobic activity a day. This includes team sports, running, swimming, fast walking, dancing or martial arts. Like cooking, this could be something you can all enjoy together.

BREAKFASTS & BRUNCHES

← LEFT, COCO-CHERRY GRANOLA. RECIPE ON PAGE 17.

BREAKFAST CEREALS, PARTICULARLY THOSE AIMED AT CHILDREN, ARE NOTORIOUSLY HIGH IN SUGAR, WHILE HEALTHY ALTERNATIVES THAT ALSO TASTE GOOD CAN BE TRICKY TO FIND. THIS MAY NOT IMMEDIATELY SPRING TO MIND AS BEING CHILD-FRIENDLY, BUT BECAUSE THE MUESLI IS SOAKED OVERNIGHT, THE OATS AND CHIA BECOME LOVELY AND SOFT AND CREAMY.

OAT AND CHIA BIRCHER MUESLI

Serves 4
**Preparation time: 15 minutes,
plus soaking overnight**

4 large handfuls of rolled oats
 or quinoa flakes
2 tbsp chia seeds, preferably
 white ones
2 tbsp sunflower seeds
600ml/21fl oz/2½ cups drinking
 coconut milk or milk of
 choice, plus extra to serve
½ tsp ground cinnamon
2 tbsp ground linseeds/flaxseeds
 or hemp seeds
2 pears

TO SERVE:
favourite fresh fruit or chopped
 dried fruit (optional)
chopped nuts and seeds
 (optional)

1 Put the oats, chia seeds, sunflower seeds and coconut milk in a mixing bowl and stir to make sure everything is submerged. Cover with a plate and leave to soak overnight in the refrigerator.

2 The following morning, stir in the cinnamon and linseeds/flaxseeds. Leaving the skin on, core and grate the pears and stir them in, then divide the mixture among four serving bowls.

3 Top with extra milk and your favourite fresh or dried fruit as well as chopped nuts and seeds before serving, if you like.

HERO FOOD

CHIA SEEDS
The chia seeds really up the nutritional value of this bircher muesli. For their size, chia seeds pack a powerful punch: not only are they a rich plant source of omega-3 fatty acids, they are also a complete protein and high in fibre. Soaking the seeds before use is said to increase their bioavailability.

FOR SOME CHILDREN, PORRIDGE/OATMEAL MADE WITH OATS CAN
BE TOO 'BITTY'. IF SO, THEN SMOOTH-TEXTURED, OLD-FASHIONED
OATMEAL/STEEL-CUT OATS COULD BE THE PERFECT ALTERNATIVE.
I LIKEN IT TO A HUG IN A BOWL AS IT'S NURTURING, SUSTAINING AND
WARMING. YOU COULD BOOST THE NUTRIENT COUNT FURTHER BY
ADDING FRUIT AND GROUND LINSEEDS/FLAXSEEDS AND HEMP SEEDS.

APRICOT & CARROT OATMEAL

Serves 4
Preparation time: 10 minutes
Cooking time: 25 minutes

165g/5¾oz/1¼ cups medium
   oatmeal/steel-cut oats

1 carrot, finely grated

10 unsulphured soft dried
   apricots, finely chopped

1 tsp freshly grated nutmeg or
   ground cinnamon

100ml/3½fl oz/scant ½ cup almond
   milk or milk of choice, plus
   extra to serve

1 heaped tsp ground linseeds/
   flaxseeds or hemp seeds
   (or both) (optional)

2 handfuls of blueberries or your
   favourite fruit

2 tbsp chopped nuts or seeds
   of choice

1 Pour 1.8l/63fl oz/7½ cups just-boiled water into a saucepan
and return to the boil. When the water is gently bubbling,
gradually pour in the oatmeal, stirring continuously to prevent
any lumps forming – don't worry if lumps do appear, just
squish them against the side of the pan with a wooden spoon.

2 Tip in the grated carrot and chopped apricots, stir, then
turn the heat down to low and cook the oatmeal, stirring
continuously, for 20 minutes. Add half the nutmeg and the
almond milk. Continue to cook, stirring, for another 5 minutes
until the grains have softened to a smooth and creamy
consistency and the apricots are soft and squidgy – add
a splash more water or milk if the oatmeal is too thick.

3 Stir in the linseeds/flaxseeds, if using, and spoon the
oatmeal into four serving bowls. Serve topped with the
blueberries, the remaining nutmeg and chopped nuts
or seeds. Top with more milk, if you like.

HERO FOOD

OATMEAL/STEEL-CUT OATS
Oatmeal/steel-cut oats is pretty much as nature
intended and so retains much of its nutritional
value, including soluble fibre, iron, calcium and
B vitamins.

THIS COCO-CHERRY GRANOLA IS MY ATTEMPT TO LURE KIDS AWAY FROM THOSE SUPER-SUGARY, SHOP-BOUGHT CEREALS. IT'S PACKED WITH NUTRITIOUS INGREDIENTS AND KEEPS SMALL TUMMIES FULL UP UNTIL LUNCHTIME. FEEL FREE TO CHOP AND CHANGE THE MIX OF NUTS, SEEDS AND GRAINS DEPENDING ON PERSONAL FAVOURITES. IF YOU DON'T HAVE JUMBO OATS, YOU CAN USE ROLLED OATS INSTEAD.

COCO-CHERRY GRANOLA

Makes about 10 servings
Preparation time: 10 minutes
Cooking time: 30 minutes

125g/4½oz/heaped 1⅓ cups jumbo oats

125g/4½oz/1¼ cups quinoa flakes or buckwheat or millet flakes (or extra oats)

100g/3½oz/scant 1 cup pecan nuts

50g/1¾oz/⅓ cup hazelnuts or walnuts

100g/3½oz/heaped ¾ cup sunflower seeds

2 tsp ground cinnamon

80ml/2½fl oz/⅓ cup melted coconut or sunflower oil

1 tsp vanilla extract

125ml/4fl oz/½ cup maple syrup or clear honey

40g/1½oz/⅓ cup desiccated/dried shredded coconut

2 tbsp unsweetened cocoa powder or raw cacao powder

100g/3½oz/heaped ¾ cup dried cherries, chopped if large

thick plain live yogurt, milk and fresh fruit, to serve

1 Preheat the oven to 170°C/325°F/Gas 3. Tip the oats, quinoa flakes, nuts, seeds and cinnamon into a large mixing bowl.

2 Mix together the coconut oil with the vanilla extract and maple syrup. Pour into the bowl containing the oat mixture and stir well until everything is mixed together. Tip the granola mixture into two baking pans, spreading it out into an even layer, then bake for 20 minutes.

3 Remove the pans from the oven and stir in the coconut and unsweetened cocoa powder until well combined. Put the baking pans back in the oven, swapping them round, for another 10 minutes until light golden. Remove from the oven, mix in the cherries and leave to cool and crisp up.

4 Serve the granola with yogurt, milk and your favourite fruit – strawberries or raspberries are a winner. The remaining granola will keep for up to 2 weeks in an airtight container.

↪ Pictured on page 12.

HERO FOOD

CINNAMON
Not only is it naturally sweet, studies have found the spice has a regulating effect on blood-sugar levels.

PERFECT IF TIME IS AGAINST YOU, THIS GRANOLA IS MUCH QUICKER
TO MAKE THAN REGULAR BAKED VERSIONS. IT'S ALSO JUST THE
THING FOR A QUICK STANDBY DESSERT: SPRINKLE IT OVER FRUIT
FOR A NUTRITIOUS NO-BAKE CRUMBLE, OVER ICE CREAM OR YOGURT,
OR USE AS A BASE FOR CEREAL BARS. IF YOU DON'T HAVE JUMBO OATS,
YOU CAN USE ROLLED OATS INSTEAD.

ONE-PAN GRANOLA

Makes about 6 servings
Preparation time: 5 minutes
Cooking time: 12 minutes

60g/2¼oz/⅔ cup jumbo oats

40g/1½oz/⅓ cup mixed seeds, such as sunflower, sesame and pumpkin

75g/2½oz/heaped ½ cup mixed unsalted nuts, such as pecans, walnuts, almonds and cashew nuts

1 heaped tsp coconut oil

1 tbsp clear honey or maple syrup

TO SERVE:

1 handful of fresh fruit per serving, such as pear, apple, peach, nectarine, strawberries or raspberries

ground hemp seeds or linseeds/flaxseeds (optional)

thick plain live yogurt

1 Tip the oats into a large, dry frying pan and toast over a medium-low heat for 4 minutes, shaking the pan occasionally, until the oats start to turn golden. (Keep an eye on them as they can burn.) Tip the oats into a mixing bowl.

2 Add the seeds to the pan and cook for 2 minutes, or until lightly toasted, stirring occasionally. Tip the seeds into the bowl with the oats, then add the nuts to the pan and toast for 4 minutes, shaking occasionally, until starting to colour.

3 Return the oats and seeds to the nuts in the pan and add the coconut oil and honey, stirring until well mixed together. Cook, stirring often, for 2 minutes until golden and slightly crisp. Tip onto a large plate and leave to cool and crisp up further.

4 Prepare your favourite fruit, as needed, and place in a glass or bowl. Top with hemp seeds, if using, then yogurt and a good sprinkling of the granola. Any leftover granola will keep for up to 2 weeks stored in an airtight container.

HERO FOOD

SUNFLOWER SEEDS
The tear-shaped sunflower seed is an excellent source of the antioxidant vitamin E. A handful makes a quick and easy snack.

PERFECT COMFORT FOOD, THIS WARMING DISH CAPTURES THE
FLAVOURS OF A CLASSIC APPLE CRUMBLE AND IS A GOOD WAY OF
ADDING FRUIT TO BREAKFAST. ANY LEFTOVER PORRIDGE/OATMEAL
CAN BE TURNED INTO SNACK BARS: SIMPLY SPREAD IT OUT ABOUT
1CM/½ IN THICK AND LEAVE TO COOL. CUT INTO BARS, THEN FRY
IN A LITTLE COCONUT OIL UNTIL GOLDEN – DELICIOUS!

APPLE CRUMBLE PORRIDGE

Serves 4
Preparation time: 5 minutes
Cooking time: 15 minutes

200g/7oz/heaped 2 cups rolled
    oats, or a mix of flaked
    grains including quinoa
    and buckwheat

300ml/10½fl oz/1¼ cups almond
    milk or milk of choice, plus
    extra to serve

2 small apples, with skins,
    cored and grated

1 heaped tsp ground mixed/
    apple pie spice, plus extra
    to serve

a few spoonfuls of One-Pan
    Granola (see page 18) or
    ready-made granola, to serve

1 Put the oats and milk in a saucepan with 900ml/31fl oz/
scant 4 cups water and bring to the boil over a medium heat.

2 Add the apples and spice to the pan, turn the heat down
to low and simmer for 10 minutes, or until the oats are cooked
and creamy. Stir continuously with a wooden spoon to stop
the porridge/oatmeal sticking to the bottom of the pan.

3 Spoon into serving bowls, pour over a little extra milk,
if you like, and sprinkle with extra spice and a good spoonful
of the granola.

HERO
FOOD

OATS
A recent study found that youngsters
who regularly eat oats are 50 per cent
less likely to be overweight. As well
as providing filling fibre, whole grains,
such as oats, surprisingly contain 25 per
cent more protein than refined cereals –
a winning combination.

QUICK IDEAS

THINGS TO GO ON TOP

QUICK, NUTRITIOUS AND SIMPLE, THESE EASY IDEAS MAKE GREAT-TASTING TOPPINGS FOR TOAST, CRACKERS, BREAD, YOGURT, FRUIT OR CEREAL. THEY ALSO MAKE A REFRESHING ALTERNATIVE TO SHOP-BOUGHT NUT BUTTERS, JAMS/CONSERVES AND SPREADS AND ARE COMPLETELY FREE FROM ADDITIVES AND REFINED SUGAR.

RECIPES SERVE 2–4.

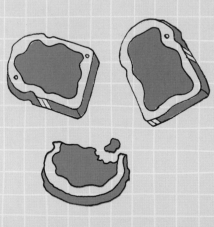

QUICK STRAWBERRY JAM

This no-cook jam/conserve takes minutes to make and relies on chia seeds as a thickener. Chia seeds are pretty amazing, super-nutritious and packed with protein, and swell impressively into a jelly-like consistency when soaked so are great for using as a thickener or as an alternative to eggs in cakes.

▷ Using a stick/immersion blender, blitz **225g/8oz/2¼ cups ripe hulled strawberries** to a purée. Spoon the strawberry purée into a bowl and stir in **2 teaspoons chia seeds, preferably white,** and **½ teaspoon vanilla extract**. Leave for 15 minutes, stirring occasionally, until thickened to a jam/conserve consistency. The jam/conserve will keep for 2–3 days stored in an airtight container in the refrigerator.

PEACH SPREAD

You can't beat the wonderful flavour of a ripe peach and by cooking it down into a thick paste you are harnessing that lovely sweet juiciness into a delicious spread for toast or a fruity topping for yogurt or porridge/oatmeal. You could also use nectarines to make the spread.

⇨ Put **4 skinned, pitted and chopped peaches** in a small pan with **1 peeled, cored apple**, **2 tablespoons water** and **1 teaspoon vanilla extract**. Cover with a lid and simmer over a low heat for 40 minutes, stirring occasionally to prevent the fruit sticking to the bottom of the pan, until cooked down to a thick paste. Blend the fruit using a stick/immersion blender until smooth, then spoon into a bowl and leave to cool. The spread will keep for 2–3 days stored in an airtight container in the refrigerator.

BIG NUT BUTTER

Shop-bought nut butters can be loaded with unwanted additives, such as palm oil, sugar and salt. But it's easy to make your own using your favourite nuts. I like to roast the nuts first to give a greater depth of flavour to the butter, but this step isn't essential.

⇨ Preheat the oven to 180°C/350°F/Gas 4. Tip **100g/3½oz/heaped ¾ cup cashew nuts** and **100g/3½oz/¾ cup hazelnuts** into a large baking pan and roast, turning once, for 12 minutes, or until the nuts start to colour and smell toasted.

⇨ Tip the nuts into a food processor and process until very finely chopped. Add **1 tablespoon good-quality sunflower oil** and continue to process the nuts until they turn into a smooth, thick paste. This takes some time and patience and you may need to occasionally scrape the nuts down the sides of the processor – depending on your processor, it will take about 10 minutes. The butter will keep for up to 1 week stored in an airtight container in the refrigerator.

CHOC-NUT BUTTER

This is a big hit in our house. A healthier version of the popular nut and chocolate spread, it uses the Big Nut Butter, left, as a base but you could use ready-made hazelnut or almond butter.

⇨ The recipe makes a relatively modest amount, so you could increase quantities to make in bulk. Mix together **4 tablespoons Big Nut Butter** with **2 teaspoons coconut oil**, **2 teaspoons clear honey** or **maple syrup**, **2 teaspoons raw cacao** or **unsweetened cocoa powder**, and **½ teaspoon ground cinnamon** (optional). Taste and add more coconut oil, cacao or honey, if you like. The choc-nut butter will keep for up to 1 week stored in an airtight container in the refrigerator.

MISO BUTTER

A great alternative to overly salty yeast extract, this nutrient-rich miso butter can be made with regular cows' or goats' milk butter or coconut oil. The nutritional yeast flakes and ground linseeds/flaxseeds boost the B vitamin and omega-3 content, respectively, but are both optional, so try it with and without and see which you prefer.

⇨ Simply mix together **30g/1oz/2 tbsp softened butter** with **1 tablespoon dark brown rice miso**, **2 teaspoons nutritional yeast flakes** and **1 teaspoon ground linseeds/flaxseeds** in a bowl. Spread the miso butter over toast or bread – it's also delicious spooned over cooked vegetables. The butter will keep for up to 1 week stored in an airtight container in the refrigerator.

THANKS TO ITS NEUTRAL FLAVOUR, TOFU – ALSO KNOWN AS BEANCURD – IS ONE OF THOSE INGREDIENTS THAT LENDS ITSELF TO BOTH SWEET AND SAVOURY DISHES. THESE SAVOURY, AMERICAN-STYLE PANCAKES TEAM TOFU WITH CORN, BUT YOU COULD REPLACE THE LATTER WITH HERBS, SPINACH, LIGHTLY COOKED BROCCOLI OR CAULIFLOWER, OR WHATEVER ELSE APPEALS – JUST MAKE SURE IT'S FINELY CHOPPED AND NOT TOO WET IN TEXTURE.

TOFU AND CORN PANCAKES

Serves 4
Preparation time: 15 minutes, plus resting
Cooking time: 30 minutes

2–3 corn-on-the-cobs, husks removed, or 250g/9oz/scant 2 cups kernels

250g/9oz tofu/beancurd, drained well, patted dry, and coarsely grated

6 spring onions/scallions, thinly sliced

175g/6oz/scant 1½ cups spelt or plain/all-purpose flour

½ tsp sea salt

2 tsp baking powder

2 large eggs, lightly beaten

270ml/9½fl oz/scant 1¼ cups milk of choice

coconut oil or butter, for frying

TRY SERVING WITH:
• eggs (cooked your favourite way)
• tomatoes or mushrooms
• veggie bacon
• Fresh Tomato Sauce (see page 101)

1 Stand a corn cob upright on a chopping board and carefully slice away the kernels. Repeat with the rest of the corn cobs.

2 Put the corn in a bowl with the tofu/beancurd, spring onions/scallions, flour, salt and baking powder and stir until combined. Make a well in the middle.

3 Whisk together the eggs and milk in a jug/measuring cup. Gradually pour the egg mixture into the tofu/beancurd mixture, stirring well with a wooden spoon until combined into fairly thick batter. Leave to rest for 20 minutes.

4 Pour enough oil into a large frying pan to generously coat the bottom and heat over a medium heat. Spoon ladlefuls of the batter, about 3 tablespoons per pancake, into the pan and cook in batches for 2–3 minutes on each side until set and golden. Turn the heat down slightly if the outside of the pancakes browns too quickly without the insides getting a chance to cook through. The batter will make 12–14 pancakes in all.

5 Serve the pancakes with your favourite toppings or simply spread with nut butter, butter or coconut oil.

HERO
FOOD

TOFU/BEANCURD

Tofu/beancurd is a good source
of calcium and iron, which makes it
particularly important for non-meat
eaters as a vegetarian diet can be
low in the latter. Iron is vital for
good physical and mental health.

THE BEAUTY OF THESE IS THAT YOU CAN QUITE EASILY COOK LOTS AT A TIME, SO THEY'RE PERFECT IF MAKING BREAKFAST FOR A LARGE FAMILY, GUESTS OR FRIENDS – AND THEY LOOK FUN, TOO. I'VE PUT GARLIC MUSHROOMS IN THE BASE OF EACH ROLL OR 'CUP', BUT YOU COULD FILL THEM WITH OTHER VEG OR SERVE PLAIN, IF YOU PREFER.

EGG CUPS

Serves 4
Preparation time: 10 minutes
Cooking time: 25 minutes

1 tbsp olive oil, plus extra for brushing

140g/5oz mushrooms, chopped

1 large garlic clove, finely chopped

4 crusty rolls, preferably wholegrain

4 large eggs

1 tbsp snipped chives (optional)

1 Preheat the oven to 180°C/350°F/Gas 4. Lightly brush a baking sheet with oil.

2 Heat the oil in a frying pan over a medium heat. Fry the mushrooms for 5 minutes, stirring regularly, until there is no trace of liquid and they start to colour. Stir in the garlic and cook for another 1 minute.

3 Meanwhile, slice off the top third of each roll to make a lid. Pull out most of the crumbs inside to leave a 1cm/½in-thick shell (saving the breadcrumbs for another recipe). Brush the rolls and lids all over, inside and out, with more oil and place the rolls on the baking sheet.

4 When the mushrooms are ready, divide them evenly among the hollowed-out rolls. Crack an egg into each one. Brush the yolks with a little oil, then bake for 5 minutes. Put the roll lids on the baking sheet and return it to the oven for another 15 minutes until the egg whites are set and the lids are crisp. Serve the egg cups with their lids by the side. You could sprinkle a few chives over the eggs before serving, if you like.

HERO FOOD

OLIVE OIL
Olive oil contains high levels of antioxidants and beneficial monounsaturated fats, which support the health of the heart.

A PERFECT WEEKEND BRUNCH . . . ALTHOUGH I'VE BEEN KNOWN TO
SERVE THESE SCRAMBLED-EGG-FILLED TORTILLAS AS AN AFTER-SCHOOL
SNACK OR EVEN AS A WEEKDAY MEAL, MADE MORE SUBSTANTIAL WITH
A SIDE OF REFRIED BEANS, GUACAMOLE AND A SALAD.

BREAKFAST BURRITOS

Serves 4
Preparation time: 10 minutes
Cooking time: 5 minutes

olive oil, for brushing
4 large seeded wholegrain tortillas
60g/2¼oz/4 tbsp butter
4 spring onions/scallions, thinly
    sliced
1 red pepper, deseeded and diced
4 tomatoes, deseeded and chopped
1 tsp turmeric
½ tsp cumin seeds
1 tsp paprika
8 large eggs, lightly beaten
60g/2¼oz Cheddar cheese, grated

TRY TOPPING WITH:
• chopped roasted peanuts
• mashed avocado and herbs
• grated raw courgette/zucchini
• Tahini-Miso Dressing
    (see page 132)
• sundried tomato pesto
• chunks of mozzarella or
    pan-fried halloumi cheese

1 Lightly oil a large frying pan and warm over a medium heat. Place 2 of the tortillas in the pan on top of one another and cook for 2 minutes, turning once, until one side of each tortilla is starting to turn golden. Place them in a low oven while you repeat with the remaining tortillas, putting them in the oven when they're ready.

2 Meanwhile, melt the butter in a non-stick saucepan over a medium heat and sauté the spring onions/scallions and red pepper for 1 minute, stirring occasionally. Add the tomatoes and cook for another 1 minute.

3 Beat the spices into the eggs and pour them into the pan containing the vegetable mixture. Turn the heat down to low and cook for about 3 minutes, gently folding and turning the eggs until lightly scrambled.

4 To serve, place each warm tortilla, golden-side down, on a plate, then scatter the cheese over each one and spoon the scrambled egg down the middle. Add additional toppings of your choice, if you like. Roll the tortillas over into a cylinder shape and cut each one in half on the diagonal, then serve.

TURMERIC

The active ingredient in turmeric, known as curcumin, has been found to benefit the brain, immune system and joints as well as reduce the risk of some cancers.

THIS MAKES A REFRESHING CHANGE FROM REGULAR BAKED BEANS
AND ALSO USES UP ANY COOKED POTATOES OR VEG YOU MAY HAVE.
THE BEANS ARE DELICIOUS TOPPED WITH A SOME GRATED CHEDDAR,
BUT OTHER CHEESES – SUCH AS FETA, HALLOUMI OR SOFT CHEESE –
ARE GOOD, TOO, AS IS A POACHED EGG WITH A DOLLOP OF HOUMOUS OR
GUACAMOLE, TRANSFORMING THE HASH INTO A QUICK WEEKDAY MEAL.

SMOKY BEAN HASH

Serves 4
Preparation time: 10 minutes
Cooking time: 10 minutes

1 tbsp olive oil

250g/9oz cooked new potatoes
   in their skins, quartered if
   large

125g/4½oz canned haricot/navy
   beans or beans of choice,
   drained

2 large handfuls of finely
   chopped cooked white
   cabbage or other leftover
   cooked vegetables

2 garlic cloves, chopped

4 tomatoes, chopped

1 tsp sweet smoked paprika

1 rounded tsp blackstrap
   molasses

2 handfuls of grated mature/
   sharp Cheddar cheese

freshly ground black pepper

1 Heat the oil in a large frying pan over a medium heat.
Add the cooked potatoes and fry for 5 minutes, turning often,
until starting to turn golden.

2 Add the beans, cabbage, garlic, tomatoes, paprika and
molasses to the pan and cook for 5 minutes, stirring often,
until everything is heated through. Stir in a splash of water
if the mixture is too dry, and heat through. Season with
pepper and serve topped with Cheddar.

TOMATOES

Tomatoes are packed with goodness,
especially vitamin C and beta carotene,
as well as lycopene, which is good for
the health of the eyes and the bones.
The latter is more bioavailable when
the tomatoes are cooked.

THESE MINI SPANISH TORTILLAS ARE COOKED IN A MUFFIN PAN.
THEY CAN BE PREPARED IN ADVANCE AND WILL HAPPILY KEEP IN
THE REFRIGERATOR FOR UP TO 3 DAYS. YOU CAN EAT THEM COLD OR
WARM (WRAP IN FOIL AND REHEAT IN THE OVEN) AND THEY CAN BE
TURNED INTO A MORE SUBSTANTIAL MEAL WITH THE ADDITION OF
A SIDE OF VEG OR SALAD, BEANS AND A TOPPING OF GRATED CHEESE.

MINI TORTILLAS

Serves 4
Preparation time: 10 minutes
Cooking time: 30 minutes

2 tbsp olive oil, plus extra for
  greasing
350g/12oz floury potatoes, such
  as Maris Piper, peeled and
  cut into 5mm/¼in cubes
½ red pepper, deseeded
  and diced
2 spring onions/scallions, white
  and green parts separated,
  finely chopped
6 eggs, lightly beaten
25g/1oz Parmesan cheese,
  finely grated
sea salt and freshly ground
  black pepper

1 Heat the oil in a frying pan over a medium heat. Add
the potatoes, turn the heat down slightly and sauté gently,
covered, for 10 minutes, turning often, until tender and
starting to colour. Add the red pepper and the white parts of
the spring onions/scallions and cook for another 2 minutes,
turning occasionally.

2 Meanwhile, preheat the oven to 180°C/350°F/Gas 4 and
liberally grease four holes of a large, deep muffin pan and line
the base of the holes with a round of baking parchment.

3 Lightly beat the eggs in a mixing bowl and stir in the green
parts of the spring onion/scallions, the Parmesan and the
cooked potato mixture. Season with salt and pepper.

4 Spoon the egg mixture into the prepared muffin pan and
bake for 18–20 minutes until risen and just cooked. (You could
also use a regular-size muffin pan and cook the tortillas for
15 minutes.) Leave the tortillas to cool for a minute or so, then
remove from the pan. Eat straightaway or cool on a wire rack.

SPRING ONIONS/SCALLIONS
Thanks to their antibacterial and antiviral
properties, spring onions/scallions can
help to relieve the symptoms of colds,
congestion, asthma and hay fever.

SMOOTHIES AND JUICES

NOTE TO ADULT HELPERS:

Making smoothies and juices is a simple way to get your kids to try their hand in the kitchen. Introducing young ones to new kinds of fruits and vegetables can be educational and encourages them to be more open to handling and tasting previously untried fresh foods.

Smoothies can be high in sugar, but this needn´t be so. Instead, see smoothies and juices as an opportunity to boost your kid´s daily intake of fresh fruit and veg. Plus, as you include the whole fruit in smoothies, they´re getting beneficial fibre, too. To make the recipes more nutritionally complete, I´ve added, where possible, a protein element as well as a source of omega-3 fats.

These recipes are all easy enough for children to make, with a little guidance when it comes to using a knife, grater or anything sharp. Use them as foundation recipes, so let your child add their own favourite fruits or veggies.

WAKE-ME-UP-JUICE

Serves 2–4
Preparation time: 10 minutes

2 apples, with skins and cores, cut into wedges
4 broccoli florets with stalks
2 kiwi fruit, halved
2 handfuls of kale leaves, stalks removed
3 handfuls of seedless green grapes
1 handful of shredded white cabbage
a squeeze of lemon juice

▷→ Feed the apples, broccoli, kiwi, kale, grapes and cabbage through your juice machine. If your juicer struggles with the leafy greens, it´s a good idea to alternate them with some fruit to help them on their way. Add a squeeze of lemon juice, then pour the juice into glasses.

TO ADD PROTEIN TO THE JUICE, YOU COULD STIR IN A SPOONFUL OF SOY OR PEA PROTEIN POWDER.

ALMOND, VANILLA & TAHINI SMOOTHIE

Serves 2–4
Preparation time: 5 minutes,
plus soaking

500ml/17fl oz/2 cups almond milk or nut
  milk of choice
2 tbsp white or black chia seeds
2 bananas, roughly chopped
2 tsp ground linseeds/flaxseeds
2 tbsp rolled oats
1 tbsp tahini paste
4 heaped tbsp thick plain live yogurt
1 tsp vanilla extract
favourite fresh fruit, chopped if needed,
  for topping

⊵⇢ Pour the milk into a jug
and stir in the chia seeds. Leave
to soak for 10–15 minutes until
the chia soften and swell.

⊵⇢ Tip the milk mixture into
a blender with the bananas,
linseeds/flaxseeds, oats, tahini,
yogurt and vanilla and whiz
until smooth and creamy. Pour
into glasses and top with your
favourite fresh fruit.

OATY APRICOT & CARROT SMOOTHIE

Serves 2–4
Preparation time: 5 minutes,
  plus soaking

140g/5oz/scant 1 cup unsulphured
  soft dried apricots
1 small carrot, finely grated
200g/7oz/scant 1 cup thick plain
  live yogurt
2 tbsp quinoa flakes or rolled oats
1 tsp ground linseeds/flaxseeds
1 tsp vanilla extract
1 tsp ground cinnamon
clear honey, to taste (optional)

⇨ Put the apricots in a small bowl and pour over enough hot water to just cover. Leave to soften for 1 hour, or overnight if easier.

⇨ Put the soaked apricots, 4 tablespoons of the soaking water, the carrot, yogurt, quinoa, linseeds/flaxseeds, vanilla and cinnamon in a blender and blend until smooth and creamy. Taste and add a little honey, if needed. Pour into glasses and serve.

TO MAKE A CREAMY FOOL, STIR IN 1 HEAPED
TABLESPOON WHITE OR BLACK CHIA SEEDS AND
LEAVE FOR 15 MINUTES TO THICKEN. SPOON INTO
BOWLS AND SERVE TOPPED WITH PASSION FRUIT
AND ONE-PAN GRANOLA (SEE PAGE 18).

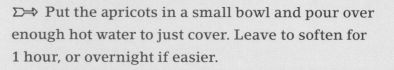

CHERRY & BEETROOT CRUSH

Serves 2–4
Preparation time: 10 minutes

200g/7oz/heaped 1 cup frozen
  pitted dark cherries
2 cooked beetroot/beets in natural
  juice
juice of 4 oranges (or 400ml/
  14fl oz/1⅔ cups fresh orange
  juice not from concentrate)
1 tsp vanilla extract
½ tsp ground cinnamon
clear honey, to taste (optional)
plain live yogurt (optional)

⇨ Put all the ingredients in a blender and blitz to a thick, smooth drink. (You may need to defrost the cherries slightly first to soften them before blending and then add some ice to the crush at the end.)

⇨ Taste and add a spoonful of honey if the crush needs to be a little sweeter. To give the crush a thick, creamy texture, add a few spoonfuls of plain live yogurt to the blender.

LUNCHES & LUNCHBOXES

← LEFT, GREEK PASTA POTS. RECIPE ON PAGE 60.

DRIED BROAD/FAVA BEANS ARE KEY HERE. THEY REQUIRE PRE-SOAKING, BUT UNLIKE OTHER DRIED BEANS THERE'S NO NEED TO PRE-COOK THEM, WHICH SERIOUSLY CUTS DOWN ON THE PREP TIME. THE BEAN BALLS ARE SERVED WITH A MINTY YOGURT DIP FOR DUNKING, BUT YOU COULD STUFF THEM INTO A PITTA BREAD OR WRAP IN A CRISP LETTUCE LEAF WITH A SPOONFUL OF THE DIP INSTEAD.

BAKED BEAN BALLS
with minty yogurt dip

Makes 16
Preparation time: 20 minutes,
    plus soaking
Cooking time: 25 minutes

200g/7oz/1 cup dried split broad/
    fava beans, soaked for
    8 hours, or 2 x 400g/14oz cans
    chickpeas, drained

3 garlic cloves, left whole

5 spring onions/scallions,
    roughly chopped

2 tbsp sunflower seeds

1 handful of flat-leaf parsley
    leaves

1 handful of coriander/cilantro
    leaves

1 tsp ground cumin

½ tsp bicarbonate of soda/
    baking soda

3 tbsp gram/chickpea flour

olive oil, for brushing

MINTY YOGURT DIP:

200g/7oz/scant 1 cup plain live
    yogurt

juice of 1 lemon

2 handfuls of finely chopped
    mint leaves or 1 tsp dried mint

1 Put the drained broad/fava beans, garlic, spring onions/scallions, seeds, herbs and cumin in a food processor and blend to a coarse paste. You will occasionally have to push the mixture down the sides of the processor to make sure everything is mixed together evenly.

2 Stir the bicarbonate of soda/baking soda and gram/chickpea flour into the bean mixture to make a thick, coarse paste – it will be slightly wet but will hold together when baked.

3 Meanwhile, preheat the oven to 180°C/350°F/Gas 4 and liberally grease a large roasting pan.

4 Using your hands, form the bean mixture into 16 walnut-size balls and put them in the prepared pan. Flatten the tops slightly, brush each one with a little oil, then bake for 20–25 minutes, turning once, until firm and light golden in places. Leave to cool if not serving straightaway.

5 While the bean balls are baking, mix together all the ingredients for the minty yogurt dip. If serving as part of a lunchbox, transfer the bean balls and yogurt to separate lidded pots.

BROAD/FAVA BEANS

Dried broad/fava beans are a great source of fibre, carbohydrate, protein, vitamins and minerals – perfect for providing sustained amounts of energy for the afternoon ahead.

KIDS LOVE FINGER FOODS AND THIS DIP IS QUICK AND EASY TO RUSTLE UP IN THE MORNING. SERVE IT WITH THE DUNKERS BELOW – THERE ARE PITTA CHIPS OR HOMEMADE SPICY TORTILLA CHIPS – OR FINGERS OF PITTA BREAD, CRACKERS OR FLATBREAD ARE EQUALLY GOOD.

FRUITY TZATZIKI
with dunkers

Serves 2
Preparation time: 5 minutes
Cooking time: 10 minutes

100g/3½oz/scant ½ cup plain live yogurt

2.5cm/1in piece of cucumber, quartered, deseeded and diced

½ small red apple, with skin, cored and grated

½ garlic clove, crushed

juice of ½ lime

freshly ground black pepper

SPICY TORTILLA CHIPS:

2 large seeded wholegrain tortillas

extra virgin olive oil, for brushing

1 tsp Mexican spice blend or other favourite spice blend

PITTA CHIPS:

1 wholegrain pitta bread

extra virgin olive oil, for brushing

1 tsp Spicy-Nutty Savoury Crunch (see page 69), or favourite spice blend

1 To make the tortilla chips, preheat the oven to 180°C/350°F/Gas 4. Put the tortillas on separate shelves in the oven for about 8 minutes, turning once, until crisp. Remove from the oven, brush one side with oil, then sprinkle the spice mix over the top. Cut into wedges, then leave to cool and crisp up.

2 To make the pitta chips, insert a small knife around the edge of the pitta to open it out, then slice it down the middle – you should now have 2 thin slices of pitta. Brush both sides of each slice of pitta with olive oil. Toast them in a large, dry frying pan for about 5 minutes, turning once, until crisp and golden. (You may need to do this in batches.) Sprinkle over the spice mix and leave to cool. Break the pitta into large pieces.

3 Mix together all the ingredients for the dip in a bowl. Spoon the dip into two pots with lids until ready to serve with your choice of dunker. The dip will keep for up to 3 days stored in an airtight container in the refrigerator.

HERO FOOD

LIVE YOGURT
Live yogurt is made by the bacterial fermentation of milk, giving it a rich, creaminess and providing probiotics that are essential for a healthy digestive system and gut.

SIMPLY DELICIOUS, THESE STUFFED CUCUMBER POTS MAKE A GREAT,
NO-FUSS ADDITION TO A LUNCHBOX. THE CUCUMBER COMES WITH
A FLAVOURED SOFT-CHEESE FILLING BUT FEEL FREE TO ADD YOUR
OWN FAVOURITE FILLING, KEEPING IN MIND THAT IT SHOULDN'T BE
TOO LOOSE OR WET SO IT STAYS PUT UNTIL YOU ARE READY TO EAT.

CUCUMBER POTS

Serves 2
Preparation time: 10 minutes

15cm/6in piece of cucumber
3 tbsp cream cheese
2 tsp nutritional yeast flakes
2 tbsp diced red pepper
2 tbsp snipped chives
a squeeze of lemon juice

1 To prepare the cucumber, cut it into 6 x 2.5cm/1in-thick
slices. Take a piece of the cucumber and, using a teaspoon,
scoop out the seeds in the middle, leaving a thin base to make
a cup shape.

2 Mix together the cream cheese, yeast flakes, red pepper,
chives and lemon juice in a bowl, then spoon one-sixth of
the mixture into a cucumber cup. Repeat with the remaining
cucumber slices and cream cheese filling. Store in a lidded
container, preferably in the refrigerator, until ready to eat.

HERO
FOOD

CUCUMBER
Crisp and juicy, cucumbers are
hydrating as they contain lots of
water – particularly beneficial for
children who tend not to drink
enough fluids. They are also a good
source of vitamin C and potassium.

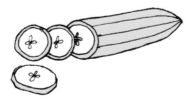

THESE MAKE A REFRESHING CHANGE TO BREAD-BASED LUNCHES AND ARE A WHOLESOME COMBINATION OF PROTEIN, CARBS, GOOD FATS AND VEG. THEY'RE EASY TO MAKE, BUT FOR MORNING SANITY ARE PROBABLY BEST PREPARED THE NIGHT BEFORE, WHICH WILL ALSO GIVE THEM THE CHANCE TO COOL. FOR A HEALTHY BOOST, WHY NOT SPLIT THEM IN HALF AND FILL WITH SOFT CHEESE, GUACAMOLE OR HOUMOUS.

POLENTA AND PEPPER MUFFINS

Makes 12
Preparation time: 20 minutes
Cooking time: 35 minutes

85g/3oz/6 tbsp butter, melted, plus extra for greasing

1 large corn-on-the cob, husk removed, or 140g/5oz/1 cup kernels

140g/5oz/heaped 1 cup spelt flour

140g/5oz/scant 1 cup instant polenta/cornmeal

2 tsp baking powder

1 tbsp ground linseeds/flaxseeds

1 tsp sea salt

284ml/10fl oz/1¼ cups buttermilk

100ml/3½fl oz/scant ½ cup milk

2 eggs, lightly beaten

60g/2oz mature/sharp Cheddar cheese, grated

3 spring onions/scallions, finely sliced

½ small red pepper, deseeded and diced

1 red chilli, deseeded and diced (optional)

1 Preheat the oven to 200°C/400°F/Gas 6. Liberally grease a 12-hole muffin pan (or line the pan with deep paper cases).

2 Stand the corn cob upright on a chopping board and carefully slice away the kernels.

3 Mix together the spelt flour, polenta/cornmeal, baking powder, linseeds/flaxseeds and salt in a large mixing bowl and make a well in the middle.

4 Whisk together the buttermilk, milk and eggs in a bowl. Pour the buttermilk mixture into the dry ingredients and add the cheese, corn, spring onions/scallions, red pepper and chilli, if using. Using a wooden spoon, gently mix until everything is combined. Spoon the batter into the prepared muffin pan and bake for 30–35 minutes until risen and cooked. Leave in the pan for a few minutes before turning out onto a wire rack to cool.

GROUND LINSEEDS/FLAXSEEDS

Golden linseeds/flaxseeds are the richest plant source of omega-3 fats, which are essential for a healthy brain, joints and heart. Not only are they easy to use when ground to a powder, the omega-3 is said to be in a more readily absorbable form.

SAVOURY SCONES/BISCUITS MAKE A GOOD ALTERNATIVE TO THE USUAL SANDWICH AND THESE HAVE BEEN PIMPED UP WITH THE ADDITION OF CHEESE, APPLE AND LINSEEDS/FLAXSEEDS. SPREAD THEM WITH BUTTER OR, TO MAKE THEM MORE FILLING, SPLIT IN HALF AND FILL WITH CREAM CHEESE AND SLICES OF CUCUMBER. TO MAKE A SWEET VERSION, LEAVE OUT THE CHEESE AND STIR IN 2 TABLESPOONS SUGAR INSTEAD.

CHEESE & APPLE SCONES

Makes 8
Preparation time: 15 minutes
Cooking time: 25 minutes

200g/7oz/1½ cups self-raising wholemeal flour, plus extra for dusting

½ tsp baking powder

1 tbsp ground linseeds/flaxseeds

50g/1¾oz/3½ tbsp chilled butter, cubed

1 apple, with skin, cored and grated

90g/3¼oz mature/sharp Cheddar cheese, grated

100ml/3½fl oz/scant ½ cup milk, plus extra for brushing

1 Preheat the oven to 220°C/425°F/Gas 7. Line a baking sheet with baking parchment.

2 Sift the flour and baking powder into a mixing bowl, adding any bran left in the sieve/fine-mesh strainer. Stir in the linseeds/flaxseeds.

3 Using your fingertips, lightly rub the butter into the flour mixture until it resembles coarse breadcrumbs. Stir in the apple and Cheddar. Gradually, stir in the milk using a fork, then bring the dough together with your hands.

4 Press out the dough on a lightly floured work surface, about 2.5cm/1in thick. Using a 4.5cm/1¾in cutter, stamp out 8 rounds. Place them on the prepared baking sheet and brush the tops with milk. Bake for 20–25 minutes until risen and golden. Transfer to a wire rack and serve warm or leave to cool completely.

HERO FOOD

APPLES

Much of an apple's vitamin C content is found within or just below the skin, so it pays to eat the fruit with the skin on. The whole fruit is also a good source of fibre and valuable antioxidants.

QUICK IDEAS

DIPS & SPREADS

MOST KIDS LOVE DIPS – ANY FOOD THAT DOESN´T REQUIRE EATING WITH A KNIFE AND FORK GENERALLY GETS A THUMBS UP! DIPS HAVE A LOT GOING FOR THEM: THEY´RE VERSATILE, EASY TO MAKE AND EAT, NUTRITIOUS AND ARE A CONVENIENT WAY OF BOOSTING FRUIT AND VEG IN THE DIET. THEY ALSO KEEP WELL STORED FOR A FEW DAYS IN THE REFRIGERATOR, SO MAKE A READILY AVAILABLE SNACK.

THESE IDEAS FOR DIPS ARE JUST CRYING OUT TO BE DUNKED INTO – SEE THE RECIPES FOR DUNKERS ON PAGE 40 – OR TRY VEGETABLE STICKS, INCLUDING CARROTS, MANGETOUT/SNOW PEAS, SUGAR SNAP PEAS, PEPPER, CELERY, COURGETTE/ZUCCHINI, CUCUMBER, BROCCOLI AND CAULIFLOWER FLORETS OR LIGHTLY COOKED ASPARAGUS.

RECIPES SERVE ABOUT 4.

RED PEPPER HOUMOUS

This version of houmous uses creamy-textured cannellini beans instead of the more usual chickpeas. It´s a simple way to encourage kids to eat pulses/legumes.

▷ Put **400g/14oz can drained cannellini beans** in a blender with **300g/10½oz/2 cups chopped roasted red peppers** from a jar, **2 garlic cloves**, **3 tablespoons tahini**, the **juice** and **finely grated zest of 1 lemon**, **1 teaspoon ground cumin** and **3 tablespoons extra virgin olive oil**. Blend everything together until smooth and creamy. The houmous will keep for up to 1 week stored in an airtight container in the refrigerator.

SATAY DIPPING SAUCE

Use this peanut sauce as a dip, spooned over noodles or mixed into stir-fried vegetables.

▷ To make, mix together **4 tablespoons peanut butter**, **1 tablespoon reduced-salt soy sauce**, **1 tablespoon hoisin sauce**, **1 tablespoon sesame oil**, **1 crushed garlic clove**, **1 teaspoon honey**, the **juice of ½ lime**, **100ml/3½fl oz/scant ½ cup coconut (drinking) milk**, **4 tablespoons water** and **a large pinch of dried chilli/hot pepper flakes** in a saucepan. Heat gently for 5 minutes until warmed through and thickened, stirring occasionally. Serve with vegetable sticks and slices of smoked tofu/beancurd. The dipping sauce will keep for up to 1 week stored in an airtight container in the refrigerator.

PEA GUACAMOLE

This pimped-up guacamole is loaded with beneficial vitamins, minerals and good fats.

▷ All you need to do is put **60g/2¼oz/scant ½ cup defrosted peas** in a blender with the **flesh of 1 large ripe avocado**, the **juice of 1½ limes** and **1 garlic clove**, then blend until smooth and creamy (or you could use a stick/immersion blender). Spoon into a bowl and dunk away. The guacamole is best eaten on the day of making.

ROASTED CARROT DIP

Roasting increases the availability of the beta carotene in carrots and also heightens their sweetness – a double whammy. Preheat the oven to 200°C/400°F/Gas 6. Cut **4 peeled carrots** into quarters lengthways, toss them in **olive oil**, then place in a roasting pan.

▷ Roast the carrots for 40 minutes, turning once or twice, until tender and starting to colour. Tip the carrots into a deep beaker with **2 tablespoons extra virgin olive oil**, **1 garlic clove**, **1 teaspoon ground coriander** and **1 tablespoon nutritional yeast flakes** (optional), then use a stick/immersion blender to blend to a smooth, thick purée. Serve as a dip or as an alternative to mashed potato. If serving as a mash, loosen the dip with a splash of milk. The dip will keep for up to 1 week stored in an airtight container in the refrigerator.

ORANGE SQUASH DIP

Packed with vitamins and minerals, this butternut squash dip is easy to make.

▷ Preheat the oven to 190°C/375°F/Gas 5. Peel, deseed and slice into chunks **450g/1lb butternut squash**, then put it in a bowl. Add **1 tablespoon extra virgin olive oil** and **1 teaspoon ground allspice** to the bowl, then turn the squash until coated in the spiced oil. Tip the squash into a roasting pan and roast for 30 minutes, turning once, until tender.

▷ Put the squash in a blender with **5 tablespoons plain live yogurt**, **2 tablespoons tahini**, **1 crushed garlic clove**, **1 tablespoon extra virgin olive oil** and the **juice of 1 lemon**. Blend to a smooth and creamy dip, adding a little warm water if the mixture is too thick. The dip will keep for up to 1 week stored in an airtight container in the refrigerator.

CASHEW & AVOCADO DIP

The nuts boost the protein content of this dip-cum-sauce.

Cover **60g/2¼oz/½ cup cashew nuts** with warm water and leave to soak for 1 hour. Drain the cashews and put them in a mini food processor or blender with the flesh of **2 avocados**, **1 garlic clove** and the **juice of 1 small lemon (or lime)**, then process to a creamy, smooth dip. Taste and add more lemon, if needed, or a splash of water, if too thick. Transfer to a serving bowl.

THESE SAUSAGE ROLLS HAVE A NUTRIENT-DENSE FILLING OF GREEN LENTILS, VEGETABLES AND YEAST FLAKES ALL WRAPPED UP IN A PUFF PASTRY CASING. YOU COULD MAKE THE FILLING UP TO 3 DAYS AHEAD OF USING, IF MORE CONVENIENT, AND THEN ASSEMBLE THE ROLLS AS AND WHEN YOU NEED THEM. THE UNCOOKED ROLLS ARE ALSO SUITABLE FOR FREEZING – SIMPLY DEFROST BEFORE BAKING.

ROCKIN' ROLLS

Makes 12
Preparation time: 15 minutes
Cooking time: 50 minutes

1 tbsp olive oil, plus extra for seasoning
1 large onion, finely chopped
200g/7oz mushrooms, finely chopped
2 large garlic cloves, finely chopped
1 tsp dried thyme
60g/2¼oz sundried tomatoes in oil, drained and finely chopped
400g/14oz can green lentils, drained well
3 tbsp nutritional yeast flakes
320g/11¼oz pack ready-rolled puff pastry
1 egg, lightly beaten
freshly ground black pepper

1 Preheat the oven to 220°C/425°F/Gas 7 and lightly grease a baking sheet.

2 Heat the oil in a saucepan over a medium heat and sauté the onion and mushrooms, stirring often, for 8 minutes until softened. Add the garlic, thyme, sundried tomatoes and lentils and cook for another 3 minutes, or until there is no trace of liquid in the pan. Season with pepper. Using a stick/immersion blender, blend the filling to a coarse paste and leave to cool.

3 Unroll the pastry and cut it in half lengthways. Divide the lentil mixture between the 2 pieces of pastry, placing it down the middle in a long sausage shape, about 2cm/¾in wide. Brush the edges of the pastry with egg and then fold the pastry over the filling. Press the edges together to seal and crimp with a fork.

4 Cut into 5cm/2in-long sausage rolls and prick the tops a couple of times with a fork. Tidy up the ends of the rolls if the filling has squished out a bit and place on the prepared baking sheet. Brush with the remaining egg and bake for 30–35 minutes until the pastry is golden and cooked through. Leave to cool slightly before transferring to a wire rack to cool completely.

NUTRITIONAL YEAST FLAKES
These nutritious golden flakes have a slightly cheesy flavour and are a rich source of B vitamins as well as protein.

THERE'S NO NEED TO MARINATE OR ADD EXTRA FLAVOUR TO SMOKED TOFU/BEANCURD, IT'S ALL BEEN DONE FOR YOU. WHAT'S MORE, IT DOESN'T EVEN NEED COOKING AND SO MAKES A SUPER-CONVENIENT, NUTRITIOUS ADDITION TO A LUNCHBOX. USE THIS VERSATILE INGREDIENT IN SALADS, SOUPS, STIR-FRIES AND NOODLE DISHES.

SMOKED TOFU PITTA POCKETS

Serves 2
Preparation time: 5 minutes

2 wholegrain pitta breads
2 tbsp plain live yogurt
2 tsp sweet chilli sauce
2 large crisp lettuce leaves,
   halved crossways
120g/4¼oz smoked tofu/
   beancurd, cut into 12 long,
   thin slices
2 small handfuls of Alfalfa
   Sprouts (see page 112),
   or other sprouted seeds

1 Warm the pitta breads in a toaster, then cut them in half crossways and open out to make two pockets.

2 Mix together the yogurt and sweet chilli sauce and spread inside the pitta pockets.

3 Fill the pockets with a lettuce leaf, slices of tofu/beancurd and the alfalfa. Leave to cool, then wrap in cling film/plastic wrap before packing in a lunchbox.

SMOKED TOFU/BEANCURD
Look for naturally smoked tofu/beancurd, rather than smoke-flavoured versions. Made from soy beans, tofu/beancurd is a versatile, low-fat, protein-rich and iron-rich ingredient.

THIS IS A CROSS BETWEEN MY CHILDREN'S TWO FAVOURITE
THINGS – PIZZA AND FRITTATA. THE FRITTATA BASE IS TOPPED WITH
A COMBINATION OF MOZZARELLA, STRIPS OF PEPPER AND RED PESTO,
BUT YOU COULD ADD YOUR OWN FAVOURITE TOPPINGS. IT MAKES
A PROTEIN-RICH ADDITION TO A PACKED LUNCH OR YOU COULD
SERVE IT AS A WEEKDAY MEAL WITH SALAD AND CRUSTY BREAD.

PIZZATA

Serves 4–6
Preparation time: 10 minutes
Cooking time: 20 minutes

6 waxy new potatoes, such as
  Charlotte, halved if large
2 tbsp olive oil
1 large onion, chopped
8 eggs, lightly beaten
1 tsp dried oregano
¼ tsp salt
¼ tsp freshly ground black
  pepper
1 small red pepper, deseeded
  and cut into thin strips
125g/4½oz mozzarella cheese,
  drained, patted dry and torn
  into chunks
6 tsp sundried tomato pesto

1 Cook the potatoes in boiling water for 10 minutes, or until
tender. Drain and leave to cool slightly, then dice. Put them
in a large mixing bowl.

2 Meanwhile, heat half the oil in a large, deep, non-stick,
ovenproof frying pan over a medium heat. Add the onion
and cook for 10 minutes, stirring often, until softened but not
coloured. Tip the onion into the bowl containing the potatoes.
Add the beaten eggs, oregano, salt and pepper and stir gently.

3 Preheat the grill/broiler to medium. Heat the remaining
oil over a medium-low heat in the frying pan used to cook the
onion, then tip in the egg mixture and gently stir until the
potatoes and onion are evenly distributed in the pan, then
cook gently for 8 minutes, or until the base is light golden.

4 Arrange the red pepper on top of the pizzata, scatter over
the mozzarella and dot with spoonfuls of the pesto. Place
the pan under the grill/broiler for 2–3 minutes, or until the
mozzarella has melted. Serve warm or cold cut into wedges.

HERO FOOD

RED PEPPER

You can enhance the absorption of iron found in
non-meat foods by eating vitamin C-rich foods,
such as red pepper, at the same time.

THIS TAKE ON CHINESE CRISPY DUCK PANCAKES USES TEMPEH, WHICH IS SIMILAR TO TOFU/BEANCURD BUT WITH A MORE SAVOURY FLAVOUR AND NUTTIER, FIRMER TEXTURE – FIND IT IN LARGER SUPERMARKETS, HEALTH FOOD SHOPS OR ASIAN GROCERS. FOR A MORE SUBSTANTIAL MEAL, SERVE WITH A NOODLE AND VEGETABLE STIR-FRY OR SALAD.

CHINESE GOLDEN TEMPEH PANCAKES

Serves 4
Preparation time: 10 minutes,
plus marinating
Cooking time: 25 minutes

400g/14oz block of tempeh
or tofu/beancurd, drained
well, patted dry and cut into
8 x 1cm/½in-thick long slices

3 spring onions/scallions,
shredded lengthways

5cm/2in piece of cucumber,
quartered, deseeded and
cut into long, thin strips

8 Chinese pancakes or crisp
lettuce leaves

1 tsp toasted sesame seeds

HOISIN MARINADE:

4 tbsp hoisin sauce, plus extra
to serve

1 tbsp sesame oil

1 tbsp reduced-salt soy sauce

1 tbsp peeled and grated fresh
root ginger

1 Mix together the ingredients for the hoisin marinade in a large shallow dish. Add the tempeh and spoon the marinade over to coat it thoroughly, taking care not to break it up. Leave to marinate at room temperature for at least 1 hour, or preferably overnight, in the refrigerator, if time allows.

2 Preheat the oven to 190°C/375°C/Gas 5. Put the tempeh on a large baking sheet and spoon any residual marinade over the top. Roast for 25 minutes, turning once, until golden.

3 Put the spring onions/scallions and cucumber on a plate.

4 Just before serving, line a steamer pan with baking parchment, then steam the pancakes for a few minutes until heated through.

5 Carefully remove the pancakes from the steamer and put on a separate plate. Remove the tempeh from the oven and place on a plate.

6 To serve, let everyone assemble their own pancakes: smear a little hoisin sauce down the middle of each pancake, top with a piece of tempeh, a few strips of spring onion/scallion and cucumber and then finally a sprinkling of sesame seeds. Fold the sides of the pancake over the filling and enjoy.

HERO FOOD

TEMPEH

A complete protein, tempeh contains all nine amino acids that are responsible for the repair and maintenance of the body's muscles, cells and tissues. It is also rich in iron and calcium.

KIDS COOK

SUPER SANDWICHES

NOTE TO ADULT HELPERS:

Making sandwiches is an easy way to get your child involved and interested in what goes on in the kitchen and help out, too. Although, admittedly, it may be a little ambitious to get youngsters involved in sandwich making first thing, here are a few quick and healthy fillings that can be knocked up in next to no time (see page 57).

For when time is not so precious, there are a couple more recipes to try. The Stuffed Chapattis are filled with a lightly spiced lentil spread based on Spicy Dahl Soup (see page 84), while the filling for the Lunchtime Rolls (see page 57) is a hidden surprise.

Wholegrain bread, rolls and wraps provide vitamins, minerals and fibre, but don't be fooled by bread that looks healthy because it's brown – it must state wholegrain or wholemeal. Also, add a filling that is a good source of sustaining protein, such as beans, lentils, cheese, egg, nut butters, seeds, tofu/beancurd and tempeh. Adding some vegetables or even fruit – be brave – to the sandwich filling further bumps up its nutritional value.

STUFFED CHAPATTIS

Serves 2
Preparation time: 10 minutes
Cooking time: 5 minutes

2 wholegrain chapattis

1 tbsp coconut oil

4 slices of paneer cheese or halloumi, mozzarella or feta

4–6 tbsp Spicy Dahl spread (see page 84, step 2) or your favourite vegetarian pâté, or 1 tbsp mango chutney

1 small carrot, grated

4cm/1½in piece of cucumber, sliced

1 small handful of Alfalfa Sprouts (see page 112) or pea shoots

⇨ Preheat the oven to 160°C/315°F/ Gas 3. Pile the chapattis on top of one another, wrap in foil and warm in the oven for few minutes.

⊐→ While the chapattis are warming, carefully heat the oil in a large frying pan over a medium heat. Add the paneer and fry it for 2 minutes on each side until starting to turn golden. If using halloumi, cook it for the same length of time (you don't need to cook the mozzarella or feta). Remove the paneer from the pan and leave to one side.

⊐→ Carefully remove the chapattis from the oven. Open the foil package and put the chapattis on a work surface. Spread the dahl over the top.

⊐→ Place the paneer down the middle. Top with the carrot, cucumber and alfalfa. Roll up the chapattis with the filling inside. Leave to cool, then wrap each one in cling film/plastic wrap if serving as part of a lunchbox. Alternatively, halve and eat while still warm.

LUNCHTIME ROLLS

Serves 2
Preparation time: 15 minutes, plus chilling

2 wholegrain crusty seeded rolls
extra virgin olive oil, for brushing
3 tbsp tomato pesto
1 handful of rocket/arugula leaves
4 slices of roasted pepper from a jar, drained
125g/4½oz mozzarella cheese, drained,
    patted dry and sliced

▷ Using a bread knife, carefully slice the top off each roll to make 2 lids. Pull out the soft bread inside, leaving a 1cm/½in bread shell. Lightly brush the inside of each roll with oil.

▷ Put the soft bread in a mini food processor and pulse until you have breadcrumbs. Mix half of the crumbs with the pesto (the remaining crumbs can be saved for use in another recipe).

▷ Place a layer of rocket/arugula in the bottom of each roll and top with a layer of the pesto crumbs and red pepper. Top with a layer of mozzarella and then the remaining crumbs and rocket/arugula.

▷ Place the roll lids on top and wrap each roll tightly in cling film/plastic wrap. Press down lightly and leave in the refrigerator for at least 30 minutes, or longer if making the night before.

SPEEDY FILLING IDEAS

▷ Mix together **2 teaspoons tahini** with **1 finely chopped date** and place in a **pitta bread** with **falafel, rocket/arugula leaves** and **Alfalfa Sprouts (see page 112)**.

▷ Grate **30g/1oz smoked tofu/beancurd** and combine with **1 small grated carrot** and **1 chopped spring onion/scallion**. Spread **houmous** over a **soft tortilla**, top with the tofu/beancurd mixture and **salad leaves** and roll up.

▷ Mix together **30g/1oz grated hard cheese**, **½ grated apple** and **1 teaspoon tomato** or **onion chutney**.

▷ Mash together **1 tablespoon nut butter** of choice, **1 teaspoon tahini** and **1 small banana**.

▷ Mix together **2 tablespoons cream cheese**, **1 teaspoon ground linseeds/ flaxseeds** and **2 chopped sunblush tomatoes**. Instead of the tomatoes, add **chopped fig** or **grated cucumber** and **mint**.

▷ Put **60g/2¼oz/scant ⅔ cup drained sundried tomatoes in oil** in a mini food processor with **1 tablespoon of oil** from the jar, **1 tablespoon tahini** and the **juice of 1 lime** and blitz to a smooth paste. Serve with **crumbled feta**.

▷ Mash **½ avocado** with **1 tablespoon lime juice** and **a few chopped basil leaves**. Serve in a **wholegrain pitta** with slices of **grilled/broiled halloumi** or **grated hard-boiled egg**.

KIDS WHO'VE TRIED NORI WHEN EATING SUSHI MAY BE OPEN TO TRYING
THE MILD-TASTING, SUPER-GOOD-FOR-YOU WAKAME SEAWEED AS
WELL. WAKAME SIMPLY NEEDS SOAKING FOR A FEW MINUTES, SO
MAKING THIS NOODLE SALAD IN THE MORNING FOR A PACKED LUNCH
IS NOT OUT THE QUESTION. IF YOU FEEL WAKAME IS A STEP TOO FAR,
YOU COULD ADD FAVOURITE VEGETABLES TO THE NOODLES INSTEAD.

SESAME NOODLES

Serves 2
Preparation time: 10 minutes
Cooking time: 5 minutes

140g/5oz brown rice vermicelli
  noodles
5g/⅛oz dried wakame seaweed
2 tsp sesame seeds
3 tomatoes, deseeded and diced
2 spring onions/scallions, finely
  chopped
5cm/2in piece of cucumber,
  quartered, deseeded and
  diced
1 handful of Alfalfa Sprouts
  (see page 112) or other
  sprouted seeds

SESAME DRESSING:

1 tbsp sesame oil
1 tbsp reduced-salt soy sauce
1 heaped tbsp light miso paste

1 Cook the noodles, following the instructions on the packet,
until tender, then drain, reserving a little of the cooking water,
and cool under cold running water.

2 Meanwhile, put the wakame in a bowl, cover with cold
water and leave to soak for about 5 minutes until softened,
then drain. Chop into small pieces, if preferred.

3 While the noodles are cooking, toast the sesame seeds in
a large, dry frying pan over a medium-low heat for 3 minutes
or until they start to turn golden. (Keep an eye on them as they
can easily burn.)

4 Mix together all the ingredients for the dressing with
4 teaspoons of the cooking water from the noodles.

5 Put the noodles in a bowl with the wakame, tomatoes,
spring onions/scallions and cucumber. Pour the dressing over
and toss until combined. Add the sesame seeds and alfalfa and
toss again before dividing between two pots with lids.

HERO FOOD

WAKAME SEAWEED
Wakame with its soft, mildly sweet
flavour is great in soups, salads and
noodle dishes. It's rich in minerals,
particularly bone-friendly calcium as
well as magnesium, iron and iodine.

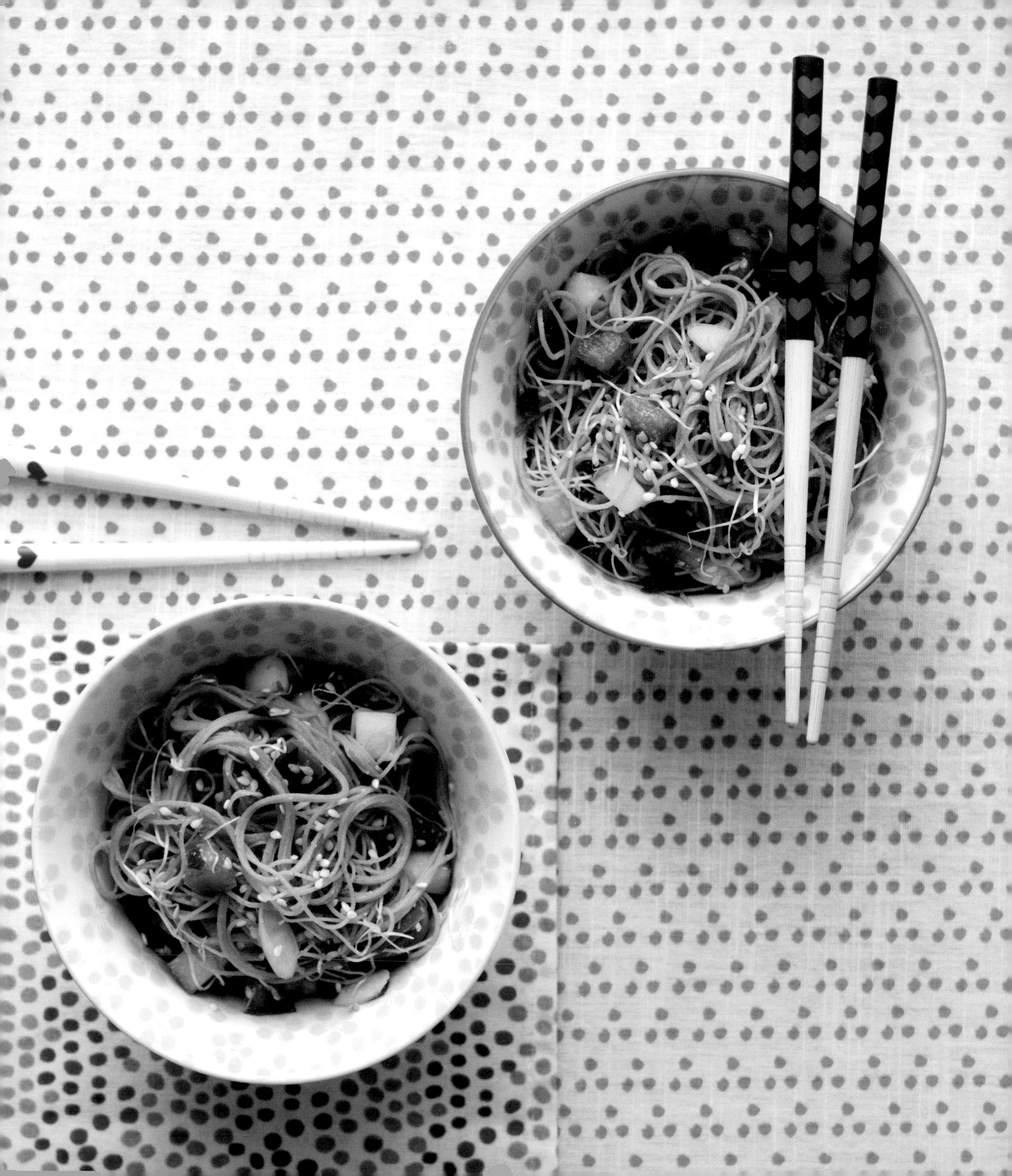

YOUNG CHILDREN DON'T TEND TO BE BIG ON SALADS, BUT I'VE FOUND IF I CUT THE FRESH INGREDIENTS INTO CHUNKY, BITE-SIZE PIECES AND COMBINE THEM WITH PASTA AND A CREAMY DRESSING, THEN THE SALAD IS A WINNER. A TWIST ON THE CLASSIC GREEK SALAD, THESE PASTA POTS COME WITH A FETA-YOGURT DRESSING, BUT YOU COULD USE MAYONNAISE OR MAYBE A FRENCH DRESSING INSTEAD.

GREEK PASTA POTS

Serves 2
Preparation time: 15 minutes
Cooking time: 12 minutes

125g/4½oz/heaped 1⅓ cups dried pasta swirls

2 tomatoes, cut into bite-size chunks

¼ red pepper, deseeded and cut into bite-size chunks

4cm/1½in piece of cucumber, cut into bite-size chunks

1 spring onion/scallion, thinly sliced

1 handful of pitted green or black olives, roughly chopped

1 handful of basil leaves, torn

1 hard-boiled egg, peeled and roughly chopped

DRESSING:

40g/1oz feta cheese

3 tbsp plain live yogurt

1 tbsp lemon juice

1 Cook the pasta, following the instructions on the packet, then drain and leave to one side to cool slightly. You could cook the pasta the night before if that's more convenient.

2 While the pasta is cooking, make the dressing. Blend together the feta, yogurt, lemon juice and 1 tablespoon water to make a smooth, creamy dressing.

3 Put the pasta in a bowl, add the dressing and turn until the pasta is coated. Add the tomatoes, red pepper, cucumber, spring onion/scallion, olives and basil and turn gently to combine. Divide between two lidded pots and scatter the egg over the top.

⇨ Pictured on page 36.

HERO FOOD

EGGS

Eggs are a brilliant addition to a vegetarian diet. Incredibly versatile, the humble egg is an excellent source of protein and altogether an excellent all-rounder.

THESE FRITTERS, WHICH COME WITH A PESTO DIP, MAKE A REFRESHING
CHANGE TO THE USUAL SANDWICH AND CAN BE MADE IN ADVANCE AND
STORED IN THE REFRIGERATOR. TRY OTHER VEG TOO, SUCH AS GRATED
RAW OR LIGHTLY STEAMED CAULIFLOWER, PEAS, CHOPPED SPRING
ONIONS/SCALLIONS OR GRATED COURGETTE/ZUCCHINI. LONG PASTA,
SUCH AS SPAGHETTI OR LINGUINE, SEEMS TO WORK BEST.

BROCCOLI FRITTERS
with pesto dip

Serves 2
Preparation time: 10 minutes
Cooking time: 5 minutes

2 eggs
30g/1oz Parmesan cheese,
   finely grated
3 lightly steamed broccoli
   florets, finely chopped
80g/2¾oz cooked spaghetti,
   roughly chopped
3 tbsp olive oil

PESTO DIP:
2 tbsp basil pesto
2 heaped tbsp mayonnaise
2 small handfuls of baby
   spinach leaves or kale
   leaves, stalks removed
2 tbsp olive oil

1 Beat the eggs in a mixing bowl and stir in the Parmesan,
broccoli and spaghetti until combined into a thick batter.

2 Heat the oil in a large frying pan over a medium heat. Put
4 x 60ml/2fl oz/¼ cup spoonfuls of the batter into the pan.
Cook the fritters for 2 minutes on each side, or until golden.

3 To make the pesto dip, put all the ingredients in a tall
beaker. Using a stick/immersion blender, blend until the
leaves are finely chopped and the mixture becomes creamy.
Spoon the dip into two separate small bowls or pots and
cover with lids.

4 Serve the fritters warm or leave to cool before wrapping
in cling film/plastic wrap for a lunchbox. Serve with the dip.

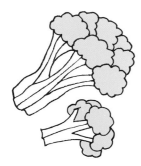

HERO FOOD

BROCCOLI
A true superfood, broccoli is loaded
with good-for-you nutrients. Alongside
a wealth of vitamins and minerals,
the vegetable, perhaps surprisingly,
provides a decent amount of protein.

AFTER-SCHOOL SNACKS

← LEFT, SWEET POTATO QUESADILLA. RECIPE ON PAGE 67.

SO EASY, SO DELICIOUS . . . THESE ARE SIMILAR TO MINI PIZZA FINGERS
BUT THE POLENTA/CORNMEAL BASE MAKES A REFRESHING CHANGE.
IT´S A GREAT WAY TO USE UP LEFTOVER POLENTA/CORNMEAL (OR USE
THE READY-MADE BLOCKS YOU CAN BUY). SIMPLY SPREAD OUT THE
COOKED POLENTA/CORNMEAL ABOUT 1CM/½IN THICK IN AN OILED
BAKING PAN, THEN LEAVE IT TO COOL AND FIRM UP BEFORE SLICING.

POLENTA PICK-UP STICKS

Serves 2
Preparation time: 5 minutes
Cooking time: 7 minutes

235g/8½oz cooked or ready-made polenta/cornmeal, cut into 6 x 1cm/½in-thick slices, patted dry

1 tbsp olive oil

1 heaped tbsp tomato purée/paste or sundried tomato pesto

½ tsp dried oregano

60g/2¼oz mozzarella cheese, drained, patted dry and torn into chunks

1 Preheat the grill/broiler to high. Meanwhile, heat a large frying pan over a medium heat. Brush one side of each polenta/cornmeal slice with a little of the oil, then place in the pan and cook for 2–3 minutes until crisp.

2 Meanwhile, mix together the tomato purée/paste and oregano with the remaining oil.

3 Carefully spread the tomato mixture over the uncooked side of the polenta slices in a thin, even layer. Top with the mozzarella and place under the grill/broiler for 4 minutes, or until the cheese has melted and is starting to turn golden. Leave to cool slightly before serving.

POLENTA/CORNMEAL
This gluten-free grain, made from corn, is ideal for those with an allergy or intolerance to wheat. It is a good source of carotenoids, which are easier to absorb by the body when combined with a source of fat, such as olive oil.

PERFECT SERVED PLAIN, THESE HIGH-FIBRE, ENERGY-PACKED OATCAKES CAN ALSO BE TOPPED WITH PROTEIN-RICH CHEESE, VEGETARIAN PÂTÉ, AVOCADO, HOUMOUS OR PEANUT BUTTER FOR A MORE SUBSTANTIAL AND SUSTAINING SNACK. A MEDIUM-GRAIN OATMEAL/STEEL-CUT OATS IS IDEAL FOR THE BEST TEXTURE AND FLAVOUR.

SEEDED OATCAKES

Makes 16
Preparation time: 15 minutes
Cooking time: 15 minutes

100g/3½oz/7 tbsp unsalted butter, diced, plus extra for greasing

100g/3½oz/scant ¾ cup medium oatmeal/steel-cut oats

165g/5¾oz/heaped 1 cup wholegrain flour, plus extra for dusting

1 tbsp ground linseeds/flaxseeds

2 tsp baking powder

¼ tsp sea salt

2 tbsp sunflower seeds

4 tbsp milk

1 Preheat the oven to 200°C/400°F/Gas 6. Lightly grease two baking sheets.

2 Mix together the oatmeal/oats, flour, ground linseeds/flaxseeds, baking powder and salt in a mixing bowl.

3 Using your fingertips, lightly rub the butter into the flour mixture until it resembles fine breadcrumbs. Stir in the sunflower seeds. Pour in the milk and mix with a fork, then use your hands to form the mixture into a dough.

4 Turn the dough out onto a lightly floured work surface and knead briefly until smooth. Using a floured rolling pin, roll out the dough into a rectangle about 5mm/¼in thick. Trim the edges and cut into 16 squares, re-rolling any trimmings as necessary. Put the oatcakes on the prepared baking sheets and prick the top of each one a couple of times with a fork.

5 Bake for 15 minutes until light golden, swapping the sheets halfway. Place on a wire rack to cool.

OATMEAL
Oatmeal provides fibre as well as complex carbohydrates, which are a source of energy in the body.

A GREAT WAY TO USE UP LEFTOVER BAKED SWEET POTATO, PUMPKIN OR SQUASH, THIS 'TORTILLA SANDWICH' MAKES A QUICK, FILLING SNACK. ALTERNATIVE FILLING IDEAS INCLUDE MASHED COOKED LENTILS WITH SHREDDED SPINACH OR KALE, LEMON ZEST AND GRATED CHEESE, OR TRY A MIX OF CRUSHED BEANS, SWEETCORN, AVOCADO AND TOMATO WITH SOFT CHEESE AND FAJITA SPICES.

SWEET POTATO QUESADILLA

Serves 1–2
Preparation time: 5 minutes
Cooking time: 6 minutes

1 small baked sweet potato, halved and flesh scooped out

2 large seeded wholegrain tortillas

½ small red onion, thinly sliced into rounds

70g/2½oz mozzarella cheese, drained, patted dry and sliced

1 handful of rocket/arugula leaves

a few basil leaves

olive oil, for frying

1 Mash the cooked sweet potato until smooth. Put one of the tortillas on a work surface and spread the sweet potato over in an even layer, leaving a border around the edge. Top with the onion, mozzarella, rocket/arugula and basil, then the remaining tortilla.

2 Pour in enough oil to lightly coat the base of a large frying pan and heat over a medium-low heat. Carefully add the quesadilla and press the edges together to stop the filling escaping. Cook the quesadilla for 2–3 minutes on each side, turning the heat down slightly if browning too quickly, until the outside is crisp and golden.

3 Slide the quesadilla onto a plate, leave to cool for a minute, then cut into wedges to serve.

▷ Pictured on page 62.

HERO FOOD

SWEET POTATO
Like carrots, the orange-fleshed sweet potato is high in the heart-friendly antioxidant beta carotene. It's also a good source of fibre, vitamin C and some B vitamins.

QUICK IDEAS

NIBBLES

MOST CHILDREN NEED SOMETHING TO EAT WHEN THEY GET HOME FROM SCHOOL AND A WELL-TIMED, NUTRIENT-RICH SNACK WILL BOOST FLAGGING ENERGY LEVELS AS WELL AS HELP IMPROVE CONCENTRATION AND LIFT MOOD.

SO, INSTEAD OF GRABBING FOR THE CRISPS/CHIPS, THESE SIMPLE SNACKS MAKE A HEALTHIER – BUT NO LESS TASTY – ALTERNATIVE. THERE ARE LOTS OF DIFFERENT IDEAS TO CHOOSE FROM AND MOST WILL KEEP FOR UP TO 1 WEEK, IF NOT LONGER, STORED IN AN AIRTIGHT CONTAINER.

IN ADDITION TO THESE IDEAS, A FRESH FRUIT AND VEG SMOOTHIE; VEGETABLES STICKS WITH DIPS; WHOLEGRAIN TOAST TOPPED WITH NUT BUTTER AND BANANA OR TAHINI AND CHOPPED DATES; AND CREAM-CHEESE-AND-HERB-FILLED CELERY STALKS ALL MAKE QUICK AND EASY SNACKS AND WILL CURB HUNGER PANGS UNTIL DINNERTIME.

RECIPES SERVE ABOUT 4.

HONEY-SOY ROASTED CASHEWS

Also try unsalted peanuts, pecans, almonds, hazelnuts, sunflower or pumpkin seeds.

⇨ Preheat the oven to 160°C/325°F/Gas 3. Roast **200g/7oz/1²⁄₃ cups unsalted cashews** for 10 minutes, turning once. Mix with **1 tablespoon reduced-salt soy sauce** and **½ teaspoon clear honey**, spread out on a baking sheet and return to the oven for 3 minutes until golden. Cool, then keep for up to 1 week in an airtight container.

KALE CHIPS

These are surprisingly moreish and make a delicious savoury snack sprinkled with nutritional yeast flakes – eat as they are or scatter over noodles, rice or salads.

⇨ Preheat the oven to 160°C/325°F/Gas 3. Remove the tough central stalks from **2 large handfuls of curly kale**, tear it into large bite-size pieces and scatter over a baking sheet. Add **a splash of olive oil** and toss until lightly coated. Bake for 15 minutes, turning twice, until crisp and watching it doesn't burn. Remove from the oven, sprinkle with **1 tablespoon nutritional yeast flakes,** toss until combined and serve.

MAGIC BEANS

These oven-baked, spiced pulses/legumes make a nutritious alternative to crisps/chips. Pictured on page 82.

⊳→ Preheat the oven to 180°C/350°F/Gas 4. Mix **400g/14oz drained and dried canned chickpeas** in a bowl with **1 tablespoon olive oil** and **1 tablespoon spice blend of your choice**, such as curry powder, Cajun, Mexican or Moroccan spice mix.

⊳→ Tip the chickpeas into a large roasting pan, spread out in an even layer and roast for 30 minutes, turning once or twice, or until crisp and golden. Leave to cool and crisp up further. Any leftovers can be stored in an airtight container for up to 1 week.

SPICY-NUTTY SAVOURY CRUNCH

This is a version of *dukka*, the moreish Egyptian blend of toasted nuts, seeds and spices with a hint of chilli. The savoury crunch adds a nutrient boost to all kinds of meals, from pilafs and bakes to salads and roasted veg. Alternatively, serve as a dry dip or mix into a paste with olive oil. Here, I've served it with hard-boiled eggs and vegetable sticks for a healthy snack, but you could smear it over warmed pitta bread. Any leftover crunch will keep for up to 1 month stored in an airtight container in the refrigerator.

⊳→ Put **4 teaspoons coriander seeds**, **2 teaspoons cumin seeds**, **4 tablespoons sunflower seeds** and **2 tablespoons sesame seeds** in a large, dry frying pan and toast over a medium-low heat for 2–3 minutes, shaking the pan occasionally, until they smell lightly toasted, then tip everything into a bowl to cool.

⊳→ Put **60g/2¼oz/scant ½ cup hazelnuts** in the same pan and toast for 5 minutes, shaking the pan occasionally, then leave to cool. Tip everything into a mini processor and grind to a coarse, crumbly mixture and stir in **a pinch of dried chilli/hot pepper flakes**, if you like.

⊳→ Put a few spoonfuls of savoury crunch in a small dish and either serve as it is or mix it to a paste with some **extra virgin olive oil**. Dunk **hard-boiled eggs**, **carrot** and **pepper sticks** into the nutty mix.

CORN WITH MISO BUTTER

Corn-on-the-cob makes a simple snack either cooked in boiling water or chargrilled as here (the latter gives it a lovely smoky flavour).

⊳→ To chargrill, remove the husks from the **sweetcorn** and brush with a little **olive oil**. Preheat the griddle pan over a medium heat, place the corn in the pan and cook, turning occasionally, for 12–15 minutes until tender and coloured in places. Serve topped with a spoonful of Miso Butter (see page 23).

SAVOURY POPCORN

Simple and fun, spice up homemade popcorn with ground pistachios, Cajun spices and honey.

⊳→ Heat **1 tablespoon oil**, add **85g/3oz/ ½ cup popping corn**, turn down to low, cover and shake the pan until the popping stops.

⊳→ Melt **2 tablespoons clear honey** and stir in **1–2 teaspoons Cajun spice mix**, **40g/1½oz/¼ cup crushed unsalted pistachio nuts** and **a large pinch of sea salt**. Stir into the popcorn until coated. Serve straightaway or keep in an airtight container for up to 1 day.

THE ADDITION OF GRATED RAW CAULIFLOWER ADDS A NEW AND NUTRITIOUS DIMENSION TO THE EVER-POPULAR CHEESE ON TOAST – AND WHAT'S MORE, THE CAULIFLOWER IS BARELY DETECTABLE. I'M NOT USUALLY A BIG FAN OF HIDING VEGETABLES IN DISHES, BUT SOMETIMES NEEDS MUST!

CAULI-CHEESE TOASTIES

Serves 1–2
Preparation time: 5 minutes
Cooking time: 7 minutes

2 slices of seeded wholegrain
    bread
1 large egg yolk
¼ tsp English mustard
1½ tbsp milk
50g/1¾oz mature/sharp
    Cheddar cheese, grated
2 large cauliflower florets,
    grated
butter, for spreading

1 Preheat the grill/broiler to medium-high.

2 Lightly toast one side of each slice of bread.

3 Meanwhile, mix together the egg yolk, mustard and milk in a bowl. Stir in the cheese and cauliflower, mashing the vegetable slightly with the back of a fork.

4 Remove the toast from the grill/broiler and butter the untoasted side. Spoon the cheese mixture on top and spread it out almost to the edges. Return to the grill/broiler for 5 minutes until the cheese mixture starts to turn golden in places. Leave to cool slightly before serving.

HERO
FOOD

CAULIFLOWER
Right up there in the health food stakes with broccoli and other brassicas, the humble cauliflower is a good source of fibre, vitamins C, K and some Bs as well as, perhaps surprisingly, omega-3 fats and protein.

SANDWICHES CAN BECOME A BIT SAMEY AND IT'S EASY TO GET STUCK
IN A RUT WITH FILLINGS. THIS SNACK IS BASICALLY A TWIST ON AN OPEN
SANDWICH WITH A TOPPING OF SMOKED TOFU/BEANCURD, GRATED
CARROT, SPROUTED SEEDS AND A MILDLY SPICY CURRY MAYONNAISE.

TOFU TIKKA NAAN

Serves 2
Preparation time: 10 minutes
Cooking time: 5 minutes

1 large or 2 small wholegrain naan
    breads
2 crisp lettuce leaves, shredded
1 carrot, grated
175g/6oz block of smoked tofu/
    beancurd (preferably the one
    with sesame seeds), cut into
    4 pieces
2.5cm/1in piece of cucumber,
    deseeded and grated
2 tbsp sprouted seeds (see
    page 112)

TIKKA CURRY SAUCE:
2 tsp tikka curry paste
2 tbsp plain live yogurt
1 tbsp houmous
a squeeze of lime juice

1 Warm both sides of the naan bread(s) in a large, dry
frying pan.

2 Meanwhile, mix together all the ingredients for the
tikka curry sauce.

3 Smear the warm naan breads with half of the curry sauce
and top with the lettuce, carrot, tofu/beancurd, cucumber
and sprouted seeds. Spoon the remaining curry sauce on top.
Cut into pieces, if you like.

LETTUCE
Lettuce doesn't just add crunch to
salads and other meals, it is a source
of vitamins A, B, C and K as well as
antioxidants.

YOU CAN'T BEAT CANNED BEANS (THE ONES IN TOMATO SAUCE) ON TOAST AS A CONVENIENT, SPEEDY SNACK BUT PREPARING YOUR OWN VERSION DOESN'T TAKE MUCH LONGER AND MAKES A GREAT-TASTING, NUTRITIOUS ALTERNATIVE.

BBQ BEANS ON TOAST

Serves 2
Preparation time: 10 minutes
Cooking time: 15 minutes

20g/¾oz/1½ tbsp butter
1 garlic clove, finely chopped
1 carrot, finely grated
400g/14oz can kidney beans, drained
2 tsp reduced-salt soy sauce
1 tsp balsamic vinegar
1 tbsp tomato ketchup
wholegrain toast, grated cheese (optional) or Pitta Chips (see page 40), to serve

1 Melt the butter in a medium-size saucepan over a medium-low heat, add the garlic and carrot and cook, stirring, for a couple of minutes.

2 Tip in the beans, soy sauce, balsamic vinegar and ketchup, then stir in 2–3 tablespoons water. Bring almost to the boil, turn the heat down and simmer, part-covered with a lid, for 10 minutes, or until the sauce has reduced and thickened and the beans are tender.

3 Serve the beans on toast, topped with cheese, if you like, or in a bowl with pitta chips by the side.

HERO FOOD

KIDNEY BEANS
Low in fat and a great source of protein, complex carbohydrates, vitamins, minerals and fibre – you can't go wrong with beans.

BROWN RICE PASTA IS A RELATIVELY RECENT DISCOVERY AND ITS
APPEAL IS THAT IT IS TASTY AND WHOLESOME WITHOUT BEING HEAVY
AND STODGY. THIS MAKES A QUICK AFTER-SCHOOL SNACK BUT
YOU COULD PIMP IT UP FOR A WEEKDAY SUPPER. ADD A COUPLE OF
HANDFULS OF FROZEN PEAS TO THE PASTA COOKING WATER, FOR
INSTANCE, AND THEN TOP THE FINISHED DISH WITH A POACHED EGG.

⁜SPECIAL⁜ SPAGHETTI

Serves 2
Preparation time: 5 minutes
Cooking time: 12 minutes

200g/7oz brown rice spaghetti
   (or wholegrain)
30g/1oz/2 tbsp butter
2 tsp yeast extract
1 tbsp nutritional yeast flakes
freshly ground black pepper
freshly grated Parmesan
   cheese, to serve (optional)

1 Cook the pasta, following the instructions on the packet,
until *al dente*. Drain the pasta, reserving 6 tablespoons of
the cooking water.

2 Return the pasta to the pan with half of the reserved
cooking water and place on the still-warm hob/stovetop.
Add the yeast extract and yeast flakes and toss until
combined, adding more of the cooking water to loosen
the pasta, if needed.

3 Season the pasta with pepper and serve sprinkled with
Parmesan, if you like.

HERO
FOOD

BROWN RICE SPAGHETTI
Ideal for those intolerant or allergic to
wheat, brown rice pasta contains more
fibre and a higher concentration of
vitamins and minerals than its white,
more refined alternatives.

ALL WRAPPED UP

NOTE TO ADULT HELPERS:

Not all snacks are bad, in fact they can play a positive role in boosting the quality of your child's diet and are an ideal opportunity to include the recommended five-a-day.

In addition to three meals a day, a couple of healthy, nutrient-dense snacks, containing a mix of wholegrain starches, protein, good fats and fresh fruit and veg, will keep energy levels sustained, help to boost mood, improve concentration and ensure your child gets a good range of dietary nutrients.

It's obviously much easier to control what young ones eat, but when it comes to older children and teenagers it can be tricky to monitor exactly what they are consuming outside of the main meals provided at home – a school lunch may well be a grabbed slice of pizza from the canteen – so it pays to have a stock of fresh ingredients that your child can easily turn into nutritious snacks when they get home from school.

TACO WRAPS

Serves 2
Preparation time: 10 minutes
Cooking time: 5 minutes

400g/14oz can beans such as black beans, chickpeas or borlotti beans, drained
1 small avocado, pitted, peeled and diced
3 tomatoes, chopped
¼ red onion, diced
1 handful of chopped coriander/cilantro leaves
juice of 1 lime
1 tbsp extra virgin olive oil
4 corn taco shells
1 handful of grated mature/sharp Cheddar cheese
4 tsp sour cream (optional)
a few dried chilli/hot pepper flakes (optional)

⇨ Preheat the oven to 180°C/350°F/Gas 4. Gently mix the canned beans, avocado, tomatoes, onion, coriander/cilantro leaves, lime juice and oil in a bowl.

⇨ Stand the taco shells upright in a small baking dish and warm for 5 minutes.

⇨ To assemble, spoon the bean mixture into the taco shells. Scatter the cheese over and top with a spoonful of sour cream and a few chilli/hot pepper flakes, if you like.

OMELETTE WRAPS

Serves 2
Preparation time: 10 minutes
Cooking time: 6 minutes

4 eggs
25g/1oz/2 tbsp unsalted butter
1 small avocado, halved, pitted
    and flesh mashed (optional)

VEGETABLE FILLING:

2 tsp reduced-salt soy sauce
1 tsp sesame oil
1 tsp grated fresh root ginger (no
    need to peel)
2 spring onions/scallions, cut into
    long, thin strips
½ red pepper, deseeded and cut into
    long, thin strips
2 handfuls of beansprouts

⟹ First, prepare the vegetable filling. Mix together the soy sauce, sesame oil and ginger in a bowl. Add the spring onions/scallions, red pepper and beansprouts and turn with a spoon until combined. Leave to one side while you cook the omelette.

⟹ Crack 2 of the eggs into a bowl and beat lightly with a fork.

⟹ Melt half the butter in a large frying pan over a medium heat. Pour the beaten eggs into the pan and swirl it around so that the egg covers the bottom of the pan.

⟹ When the egg begins to set, draw the edges towards the middle using a spatula, letting the raw egg run into the space. Cook for about 2 minutes, or until the egg forms a thin omelette.

⟹ Slide the omelette onto a plate and keep it warm while you make a second omelette with the remaining eggs.

⟹ Spoon the avocado, if using, down one side of each omelette, then top with the vegetable mixture. Roll up the omelettes, place on serving plates and cut each one crossways in half before serving.

NORI WRAPS

Serves 2
Preparation and cooking time: 5 minutes

2 nori sheets (the same as the ones
   used for sushi)
2 tsp miso paste (any type will do, but
   I prefer the lighter-flavoured white one)
1 spring onion/scallion, shredded
¼ red pepper, deseeded and cut into long,
   thin strips
1 carrot and/or 1 turnip, cut into long,
   thin strips
½ tsp toasted sesame seeds

TRY FILLING WITH EXTRA:
• slices of avocado
• thin strips of smoked or regular tofu/
   beancurd
• toasted sunflower, pumpkin or hemp seeds
• peanut butter instead of the miso paste
• tahini instead of the miso paste
• grated hard-boiled eggs
• cooked quinoa or brown rice

▷ Using tongs, carefully hold a sheet of nori about 4cm/1½in over a medium-low heat for a few seconds, moving the nori over the heat until it is evenly and lightly toasted and crisp. Repeat with the second sheet, then cut both diagonally in half.

▷ Smear a strip of miso down the middle of each triangle of nori. Place a few strips of spring onion on top of the miso, followed by the red pepper and carrot and/or turnip (you can add any additional fillings, if you like). Scatter the sesame seeds over and roll up the nori sheets with the filling inside – they're now ready to eat.

THESE WRAPS ARE BEST MADE JUST BEFORE

EATING, OTHERWISE THE NORI TURNS SOGGY.

WHY NOT PUT THE FILLING INGREDIENTS

IN SEPARATE BOWLS ON THE TABLE AND

LET EVERYONE HELP THEMSELVES,

ROLLING THEIR OWN WRAPS?

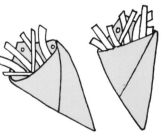

THIS PASTA BROTH IS MORE OF AN ´ASSEMBLY´ SOUP THAN ONE
THAT NEEDS LENGTHY PREPARATION AND COOKING. THIS MEANS IT´S
INCREDIBLY FLEXIBLE SO DON´T BE SHY OF ADDING EXTRA INGREDIENTS:
LEFTOVER COOKED VEG; COOKED GRAINS LIKE BROWN RICE, BARLEY
OR QUINOA; OR CANNED PULSES/LEGUMES. HOUMOUS, HARD-BOILED
EGG OR GRILLED/BROILED HALLOUMI MAKE GREAT TOPPINGS.

10-MINUTE SOUP

Serves 2
Preparation time: 5 minutes
Cooking time: 8 minutes

500ml/17fl oz/generous 2 cups
   reduced-salt vegetable stock

60g/2¼oz/⅔ cup dried alphabet
   pasta or orzo (wholegrain if
   you can find it)

2 tomatoes, deseeded and diced

1 large handful of baby spinach
   leaves

1 tbsp sundried tomato pesto

1 handful of basil leaves, torn
   (optional)

freshly ground black pepper

freshly grated Parmesan
   cheese, to serve

1 Bring the stock to the boil in a saucepan. Add the pasta, stir, then cook, following the instructions on the packet, until *al dente*.

2 Two minutes before the pasta is cooked, stir in the tomatoes and spinach. When the pasta is ready, stir in the pesto and basil, if using. Season with pepper, ladle the soup into two bowls or mugs and top with Parmesan.

PASTA

Carbs, such as pasta, have become a naughty word in some health circles, but they are an essential component of a nutritious, rounded diet, especially for children. They provide much-needed energy as well as numerous vitamins and minerals – wholegrain carbs are always best.

A HUG IN A MUG! A SPOONFUL OF BROWN MISO PASTE STIRRED INTO
A MUG OF HOT WATER MAKES A QUICK, SUPER-EASY, NOURISHING
BROTH. SERVE AS AN ACCOMPANIMENT TO ANOTHER SAVOURY SNACK
OR MAKE IT MORE SUBSTANTIAL WITH THE ADDITION OF NOODLES,
CHOPPED VEG, CUBES OF TOFU/BEANCURD, A SPRINKLING OF NORI
FLAKES AND/OR TOASTED SESAME SEEDS – GO FOR IT!

MISO NOODLE MUG

Serves 2
Preparation time: 5 minutes
Cooking time: 5 minutes

2 nests of wholegrain noodles,
    about 50g/1¾oz each
2 heaped tbsp brown rice
    miso paste

TRY ADDING EXTRA:

- 2 small handfuls of frozen
  peas (cook with the noodles)
- 2 small handfuls of frozen
  edamame beans (cook with
  the noodles)
- 1 large spring onion/scallion,
  finely chopped
- 1 small carrot, cut into
  matchsticks
- ¼ red pepper, deseeded and
  diced
- 1 tsp toasted sesame seeds
- 2 small handfuls of cubed
  tofu/beancurd
- 1 tsp nori flakes
- chopped coriander/cilantro
  or basil
- a splash of sesame oil

1 Bring a saucepan of water to the boil, add the noodles, stir
with a fork to separate the strands and cook, following the
instructions on the packet, until just tender. Drain, reserving
2 mugfuls of the cooking water, about 480ml/17fl oz/2 cups.

2 Put the noodles into two mugs (you could chop them up
first if serving to young ones). Let the cooking water cool
slightly, then pour it into the mugs over the cooked noodles
and stir half the miso paste into each mug until dissolved.
Serve straightaway or stir in your choice of extras (see left).

HERO FOOD

MISO

A jar of miso paste makes an
invaluable, convenient and nutritious
storecupboard essential. The soybean
paste (usually with added rice or
barley) provides beneficial amounts
of protein, fibre, zinc and B vitamins,
and being fermented, it supports
healthy digestion.

WEEKDAYS

← LEFT, SPICY DAHL SOUP. RECIPE ON PAGE 84 AND MAGIC BEANS, RECIPE ON PAGE 69.

GETTING MY YOUNGEST TO EAT LENTILS IS AN UPHILL STRUGGLE – YET HE WILL HAPPILY TUCK INTO THIS SOUP. IT´S VERY SIMPLE AND NOURISHING AND ALSO FORMS THE FILLING FOR THE STUFFED CHAPATTIS (SEE PAGE 54), SO YOU´RE MAKING TWO RECIPES IN ONE. PIMP IT UP WITH A TOPPING OF YOGURT, CRISPY ONIONS AND/OR MAGIC BEANS (SEE PAGE 69) AND SERVE WITH WHOLEGRAIN CHAPATTIS.

SPICY DAHL SOUP

Serves 4
Preparation time: 10 minutes
Cooking time: 25 minutes

1 heaped tbsp coconut oil or 1½ tbsp sunflower oil

1 large onion, roughly chopped

1 sweet potato, peeled and cut into chunks

2 large garlic cloves, peeled and left whole

2.5cm/1in piece of fresh root ginger, peeled and finely chopped

3 cardamom pods, split (optional)

1 tsp turmeric

140g/5oz/heaped ⅔ cup split red lentils

800ml–1l/28–35fl oz/3⅓–4¼ cups vegetable stock

1–2 tbsp mild Indian curry paste, to taste

a squeeze of lime juice

freshly ground black pepper

See introduction, above, for serving suggestions

1 Heat the oil in a large saucepan over a medium heat. Add the onion and cook, stirring often, for 5 minutes until softened. Stir in the sweet potato, garlic, ginger, cardamom, if using, turmeric and lentils until combined. Pour in the stock (add the smaller amount if planning to make the Stuffed Chapattis on page 54).

2 Bring to the boil, then turn the heat down and simmer, part-covered with a lid and stirring occasionally, for 18 minutes, or until the lentils are tender. Fish out the cardamom, then blend the soup with a stick/immersion blender until thick and smooth. (At this point, if making the dahl spread, remove 100ml/3½fl oz/scant ½ cup of the soup and transfer it to a bowl to cool and thicken.)

3 Add the remaining stock to the soup, season with pepper and warm through. Serve topped with a spoonful of yogurt, crispy onions and/or magic beans, if you like, and with a warmed chapatti by the side.

⇨ Pictured on page 82.

SPICES
The ability of spices to boost the digestive system is well known, while fibre-rich foods, such as lentils and vegetables, have similar benefits.

OMELETTES ARE A BIT OF A LIFESAVER IN OUR HOUSE WHEN TIME IS AT A PREMIUM. NOT ONLY ARE THEY QUICK AND NUTRITIOUS, THEY CAN ALSO BE FILLED WITH SO MANY DIFFERENT THINGS. THIS ONE IS BOOSTED WITH SILKEN TOFU/BEANCURD, WHICH HAS A SOFT, CREAMY TEXTURE. YOU COULD SERVE THE OMELETTE WITH A NOODLE SALAD OR RICE AND STIR-FRIED VEGETABLES.

TOFU-EGG OMELETTES

Serves 4
Preparation time: 15 minutes
Cooking time: 12 minutes

6 eggs
300g/10½oz silken tofu/beancurd, drained and mashed with a fork
5 spring onions/scallions, finely chopped
2 tsp reduced-salt soy sauce
coconut oil or sunflower oil, for frying

TO SERVE:
1 recipe quantity Fresh Tomato Sauce (see page 101)
1 tsp reduced-salt soy sauce
1cm/½in piece of fresh root ginger, peeled and finely grated

1 Lightly beat the eggs in a bowl, then beat in the tofu/beancurd, spring onions/scallions and soy sauce.

2 To make the sauce, mix together the tomato sauce with the soy sauce and ginger. Leave to one side and serve at room temperature or warmed up.

3 To cook the omelettes, heat enough oil to lightly coat the bottom of a large frying pan over a medium-low heat. Ladle a quarter of the egg mixture into the pan and spread it out into a thin, even layer. Cook for 2 minutes, or until the bottom is set and light golden, then fold in half and cook for another minute or so. (Alternatively, you could make 8 smaller omelettes and serve them flat.)

4 Serve straightaway or keep warm in a low oven while you make the remaining 3 omelettes. Serve with the tomato sauce by the side.

HERO FOOD

SILKEN TOFU
Softer in texture than regular tofu/beancurd, silken tofu/beancurd is rich in calcium and makes a useful dairy-free alternative to milk and other dairy products. It is also a good plant source of omega-3 fats and iron.

FRITTERS ALWAYS GO DOWN WELL WITH KIDS AND THEY'RE AN EASY
WAY TO INCLUDE MORE VEG – AND FRUIT IF MAKING SWEET ONES.
LEAFY GREENS ALWAYS WORK WELL AS THEY CAN BE FINELY CHOPPED,
AS DO BRASSICAS LIKE BROCCOLI, CAULIFLOWER AND CABBAGE AS THE
CHEESE IN THE FRITTERS TAMES ANY BITTERNESS. PEAS, CARROTS,
COURGETTES/ZUCCHINI AND SWEETCORN ARE ALSO GREAT ADDITIONS.

POPEYE FRITTERS

Serves 4
Preparation time: 10 minutes,
**   plus resting**
Cooking time: 20 minutes

200g/7oz/1⅓ cups wholegrain spelt
    flour or plain/all-purpose flour

1 tsp baking powder

1 tsp sea salt

200ml/7fl oz/scant 1 cup milk

2 handfuls of baby spinach leaves
    or kale, about 50g/1¾oz, tough
    stalks discarded

1 tbsp melted butter

6 large eggs, lightly beaten

60g/2¼oz mature/sharp Cheddar
    cheese, grated

1 handful of snipped chives,
    plus extra to serve

olive oil, for cooking

1 recipe quantity Fresh Tomato
    Sauce (see page 101)

crusty wholegrain bread and
    extra veg, to serve

1 Put the flour, baking powder, salt, milk, spinach and melted butter in a blender. Add 2 of the eggs and blitz to a thick batter. Leave to rest for 30 minutes, then stir in the cheese and chives.

2 Heat enough oil to coat the bottom of a large frying pan over a medium heat. Add 50ml/1¾fl oz/scant ¼ cup of the batter per pancake to the pan and cook 3–4 at a time for 2 minutes on each side until light golden. Keep warm in a low oven while you cook the remaining pancakes, adding more oil when needed – there's enough batter to make 12–14 pancakes in total.

3 Keep the pancakes warm in the oven while you fry the remaining eggs in the frying pan and warm the fresh tomato sauce. Divide the sauce and pancakes between serving plates and top with an egg. Sprinkle over the remaining chives and serve with crusty bread and favourite veg by the side, if you like.

HERO FOOD

SPELT FLOUR
Spelt is an ancient form of wheat that is growing in popularity, especially with those who find they can't tolerate regular wheat-based foods. Wholegrain spelt is full of fibre and is a good source of iron and magnesium.

THESE CHEESY BROCCOLI FRITTERS ARE CONVENIENTLY BAKED IN THE OVEN UNTIL CRISP AND GOLDEN. LEFT TO COOL, THEY MAKE A GREAT SNACK OR AN ADDITION TO A LUNCHBOX, BUT IF SERVING AS PART OF A WEEKDAY MEAL, ROASTED NEW POTATOES AND THE SUPER RED SLAW (SEE PAGE 133) WOULD BOTH MAKE GOOD ACCOMPANIMENTS. YOU COULD USE QUINOA FLAKES INSTEAD OF THE BREADCRUMBS.

BROCCOLI BITES

Serves 4
Preparation time: 15 minutes
Cooking time: 27 minutes

350g/12oz broccoli, florets and stalks finely chopped

3 spring onions/scallions, finely chopped

60g/2¼oz/1 cup day-old wholegrain breadcrumbs

140g/5oz mature/sharp Cheddar cheese, grated

2 eggs, lightly beaten

freshly ground black pepper

Super Red Slaw (see page 133) and roasted new potatoes, to serve

1 Preheat the oven to 200°C/400°F/Gas 6. Line a baking sheet with baking parchment. Steam the broccoli for 2 minutes until lightly cooked, then refresh under cold running water and drain well. Leave to dry in the sieve/fine-mesh strainer or pat dry with paper towels.

2 Mix together the spring onions/scallions, breadcrumbs, Cheddar and broccoli in a mixing bowl.

3 Make a dip in the middle of the broccoli mixture and add the eggs, season with pepper, then mix well until everything is combined.

4 Using your hands, form the mixture into 14 x 5cm/2in cylindrical pieces, then put them on the prepared baking sheet. Bake for 20–25 minutes until firm and starting to turn golden. Serve with the slaw and roasted new potatoes.

HERO FOOD

CHEESE
Dairy products play a significant part of the diets of many vegetarians and 2–3 calcium-rich portions are recommended a day for strong bones and teeth. A portion is a glass of milk or a small serving of cheese.

CHICKPEAS AND SWEET POTATOES ARE MY BEAN AND CARB OF CHOICE, BUT FEEL FREE TO GO FOR WHATEVER CANNED BEANS YOU HAVE TO HAND – HARICOT/NAVY, BUTTER/LIMA BEANS, KIDNEY BEANS OR CANNELLINI WILL ALL WORK. REGULAR POTATOES, BROWN RICE OR SEEDED FLATBREADS MAKE A GOOD ALTERNATIVE TO THE SWEET POTATO, TOO.

SWEET POTATOES
with curry beans

Serves 4
Preparation time: 15 minutes
Cooking time: 1 hour

4 large orange-fleshed sweet potatoes, scrubbed

1 tbsp coconut oil or sunflower oil

1 onion, chopped

2 large garlic cloves, chopped

2cm/¾in piece of fresh root ginger, peeled and grated

2 large tomatoes, diced

2 x 400g/14oz cans chickpeas, drained

1 tsp turmeric

1 tbsp mild curry powder, or to taste

300ml/10½fl oz/1¼ cups reduced-salt vegetable stock

1 rounded tbsp tomato purée/paste

30g/1oz creamed coconut, roughly chopped

2 large handfuls of finely chopped spinach leaves, tough stalks discarded

plain live yogurt and green veg (optional), to serve

1 Preheat the oven to 200°C/400°F/Gas 6. Bake the potatoes for 50–60 minutes, depending on their size, until tender.

2 Meanwhile, make the curry beans. Heat the oil in a saucepan over a medium heat. Add the onion and cook for 8 minutes until softened. Add the garlic, ginger and tomatoes and cook for another 1 minute, stirring.

3 Stir in the chickpeas, turmeric, curry powder, stock, tomato purée/paste and creamed coconut. Bring almost to the boil, then turn the heat down and simmer, part-covered with a lid, for 10 minutes until reduced and thickened.

4 Using a potato masher, partly mash the beans to thicken the sauce. Add a splash more water and the spinach and cook for another 2 minutes until tender.

5 To serve, cut open the sweet potatoes and serve the beans on top with a spoonful of yogurt and some veg, if you like.

HERO FOOD

CHICKPEAS
Canned beans have been found to be just as nutritious as freshly cooked ones, providing plenty of fibre, protein, iron and zinc.

EGGS ARE MY GO-TO FOOD WHEN I'M LOOKING TO COOK SOMETHING QUICK AND NUTRITIOUS. THEY'RE ALSO INCREDIBLY CONVENIENT, VERSATILE AND AFFORDABLE. THIS SIMPLE TAKE ON A SOUFFLÉ MAKES IT A SLIGHTLY LUXURIOUS WEEKDAY MEAL, WHICH IS EQUALLY GOOD SERVED WITH A SALAD AS IT IS WITH COOKED VEG.

CHEESE PUFF

Serves 4
Preparation time: 15 minutes
Cooking time: 30 minutes

10g/¼oz/2 tsp butter

100g/3½oz Parmesan cheese, finely grated, plus extra for sprinkling

200g/7oz cauliflower florets

200g/7oz broccoli florets

4 large eggs, separated

1 heaped tsp Dijon mustard

200ml/7fl oz/scant 1 cup whole milk

4 tbsp crème fraîche

new potatoes, salad or favourite vegetables, to serve

1 Preheat the oven to 190°C/375°F/Gas 5. Rub the butter inside a 29 x 23cm/11½ x 9in baking dish (or a 28cm/11in round dish) and sprinkle over 1 tablespoon of the Parmesan.

2 Steam the cauliflower and broccoli for 4 minutes, or until just tender, then remove the steamer from the heat, take the lid off and leave the vegetables to dry in the residual heat. While the veg are steaming, beat the egg yolks with the mustard, milk and crème fraîche. Stir in the remaining Parmesan.

3 Finely chop the cauliflower and broccoli into small florets and add to the Parmesan mixture in the bowl.

4 In a large, clean, grease-free bowl, whisk the egg whites to stiff peaks. Using a metal spoon, fold a large spoonful of the egg whites into the Parmesan mixture, then add the remaining egg whites, carefully folding them in so you don't lose too much air.

5 Transfer the egg mixture to the prepared baking dish, smooth the surface slightly and sprinkle the top with extra Parmesan. Bake for 25 minutes, or until risen and golden but still with a slight wobble.

HERO FOOD

EGGS

Eggs provide a range of vitamins, including A, B, D, E and K, as well as the minerals choline, iron, zinc, selenium, iodine and copper.

SO SIMPLE, SO TASTY – THIS IS OUR GO-TO SUPPER WHEN WE NEED SOMETHING QUICK AND SUBSTANTIAL AND IT TICKS ALL THE RIGHT BOXES. PORCINI STOCK/BOUILLON CUBES MAY SOUND A BIT FANCY, BUT THEY'RE A GREAT ASSET TO THE VEGETARIAN STORECUPBOARD, ADDING A RICH, SAVOURY FLAVOUR TO SOUPS, STEWS AND SAUCES. YOU'LL FIND THEM IN MAJOR SUPERMARKETS OR ITALIAN DELIS.

Favourite MUSHROOM BOLOGNESE

Serves 4
Preparation time: 10 minutes
Cooking time: 25 minutes

2 tbsp olive oil

1 large onion, roughly chopped

350g/12oz chestnut/cremini mushrooms, stalks trimmed, roughly chopped

2 large garlic cloves, finely chopped

400g/14oz can chopped/crushed tomatoes

1 porcini stock/bouillon cube

3 tbsp basil pesto

375g/13oz dried spaghetti

freshly grated Parmesan cheese, to serve

1 Heat the oil in a saucepan over a medium heat. Add the onion and sauté for 5 minutes, stirring often, until softened. Add the mushrooms and cook for another 10 minutes until they release their liquid and start to turn golden. Stir in the garlic and cook for another 1 minute.

2 Add the tomatoes to the pan with 200ml/7fl oz/scant 1 cup water and bring to the boil, then crumble in the stock/bouillon cube. Stir well, turn the heat down and simmer for 10 minutes, part-covered with a lid, until the sauce has reduced and thickened. Stir in the pesto and heat through.

3 Meanwhile, cook the spaghetti, following the instructions on the packet, until *al dente*. Drain the pasta, reserving 4 tablespoons of the cooking water, and return it to the pan. Pour the sauce over the top and turn everything until combined, adding some of the reserved cooking water, if needed. Serve sprinkled with Parmesan.

HERO FOOD

MUSHROOMS

Mushrooms are the only natural vegan source of vitamin D, and new studies have found that the benefits of vitamin D extend far wider than previously thought. Along with supporting bone health, the vitamin is now understood to support the immune system, the health of the heart, blood pressure and help with seasonal affective disorder.

THIS IS CALLED SUMMER PASTA AS IT RELIES ON GREAT-TASTING TOMATOES AND SWEETCORN, BOTH OF WHICH ARE AT THEIR BEST IN THE WARMER MONTHS. THE TOMATOES CAN BE ROASTED IN ADVANCE; IF YOU HAVE THE OVEN ON IT'S ALWAYS WORTH POPPING IN A TRAY OF TOMATOES AT THE SAME TIME TO ROAST UNTIL SOFT AND JUICY.

SUMMER PASTA

Serves 4
Preparation time: 10 minutes
Cooking time: 40 minutes

4 tbsp sunflower seeds

4 tbsp pumpkin seeds

6 handfuls of cherry tomatoes (preferably on the vine)

2 tbsp olive oil, plus extra for drizzling

2 corn-on-the cobs, husks removed, or 280g/10oz/2 cups kernels

375g/13oz/heaped 4 cups dried orzo pasta

3 garlic cloves, finely chopped

1 handful of chopped parsley leaves

freshly ground black pepper

4 tbsp shaved pecorino cheese, to serve

1 Preheat the oven to 200°C/400°F/Gas 6. Put the seeds on a baking sheet and place in the oven while it is heating up. Toast the seeds for about 10 minutes, then tip them into a bowl.

2 Put the tomatoes in a bowl and drizzle with oil to coat. Tip them onto the baking sheet and roast for 30 minutes, or until starting to collapse. Meanwhile, stand a corn cob upright on a chopping board and carefully slice away the kernels. Repeat with the second cob and set to one side.

3 Ten minutes before the tomatoes are ready, bring a pan of water to the boil and cook the orzo, following the instructions on the packet, until *al dente*. Drain the pasta, reserving 6 tablespoons of the cooking water.

4 Meanwhile, heat the olive oil in a large frying pan over a medium-low heat. Add the corn and fry for a couple of minutes until softened, then stir in the garlic. Gently stir the cooked orzo into the pan with the reserved cooking water, parsley and tomatoes, adding a little more oil, if needed. Season with pepper and serve sprinkled with pecorino and toasted seeds.

HERO FOOD

VINE-RIPENED TOMATOES
Vine-ripened tomatoes are richer in vitamin C than those picked when still slightly under-ripe – they also taste so much better!

YOU CAN'T BEAT A GOOD MACARONI CHEESE AND THIS ONE CUTS THE
USUAL LENGTHY COOKING TIME BY HALF AS IT IS MADE COMPLETELY
ON THE HOB/STOVETOP AND THEN FINISHED OFF WITH A NUTTY
SEED TOPPING. IT ALSO INCLUDES THE ADDED HEALTH BONUS OF
VEGETABLES, INCLUDING BROCCOLI, PEAS AND CABBAGE, WHICH
IS GRATED FINELY INTO THE SAUCE.

STOVETOP MAC 'N' CHEESE

Serves 4
Preparation time: 15 minutes
Cooking time: 20 minutes

350g/12oz/scant 3 cups macaroni,
   preferably wholegrain
350g/12oz small broccoli florets
140g/5oz/heaped 1 cup frozen
   peas
30g/1oz/2 tbsp butter
1 large garlic clove, crushed
3 tbsp spelt flour
500ml/17fl oz/2 cups warm milk
85g/3oz white cabbage, finely
   grated
1 tsp English mustard
250g/9oz mature/sharp Cheddar
   cheese, grated
freshly ground black pepper

NUTTY SEED TOPPING:
30g/1oz/scant ¼ cup hazelnuts
30g/1oz/scant ¼ cup blanched
   almonds
4 tbsp sunflower seeds
½ tsp dried thyme
a large pinch of dried chilli/hot
   pepper flakes (optional)

1 Cook the macaroni, following the instructions on the
packet, until *al dente*. Add the broccoli 4 minutes before the
end of the pasta cooking time and the peas 2 minutes before
the pasta is ready. Drain and leave to one side.

2 Meanwhile, make the nutty seed topping. Toast the nuts
in a large, dry frying pan for 5 minutes, shaking the pan
occasionally, until lightly coloured. Tip the nuts into a mini
food processor. Repeat with the seeds, toasting them for
2–3 minutes until they start to colour. Tip into the processor
with the nuts and grind to a coarse, crumbly mixture.
Stir in the thyme and chilli/hot pepper flakes, if using,
and leave to one side.

3 Melt the butter in a pan and stir in the garlic. Add the
flour and cook over a low heat, stirring continuously, for
2 minutes. Gradually pour in the milk, stirring, then add
the cabbage and cook for 5 minutes until the sauce has
thickened to the consistency of double cream. Stir in the
mustard and cheese and cook for another couple of minutes.

4 Stir the pasta, broccoli and peas into the sauce and heat
through, then season with pepper. Serve in bowls sprinkled
with the nutty seed topping. Any leftover topping will keep
for up to 1 week stored in an airtight container – sprinkle it
over pasta, noodles, stir-fries and salads.

THE AUBERGINE/EGGPLANT IS INTENTIONALLY CUT INTO SMALL PIECES, SO IT'S VIRTUALLY UNDETECTABLE IN THIS NOODLE DISH AND LENDS AN ALMOST 'MEATY' TEXTURE. THE RECIPE USES LONG-STEM BROCCOLI BUT YOU COULD ALSO ADD REGULAR BROCCOLI – BOTH WILL ADD A TOUCH OF COLOUR AS WELL AS GOODNESS.

AUBERGINE NOODLES

Serves 4
Preparation time: 15 minutes
Cooking time: 10 minutes

2 tbsp coconut oil or sunflower oil

1 aubergine/eggplant, cut into small dice

2 large garlic cloves, finely chopped

2.5cm/1in piece of fresh root ginger, peeled and finely chopped

1 tsp Chinese five-spice powder

1 tbsp sesame oil

1–2 tbsp reduced-salt soy sauce

4 wholegrain noodle nests, about 70g/2½oz each

200g/7oz long-stem broccoli, trimmed

1 large handful of toasted cashew nuts

½ tsp dried chilli/hot pepper flakes, to serve (optional)

1 Bring a large pan of water to the boil over a medium heat.

2 While the water is coming to the boil, heat a large wok over a high heat. Add the oil and, when hot, toss in the aubergine/eggplant. Stir-fry for 8 minutes until very tender and starting to turn golden. Add the garlic and ginger and stir-fry for another minute before adding the five-spice powder, sesame oil and soy sauce and heating through briefly.

3 Meanwhile, add the noodles to the pan of boiling water, stir to separate the strands and cook, following the instructions on the packet, until tender. Add the broccoli 3 minutes before the end of the noodle cooking time.

4 Using tongs, scoop the noodles and broccoli out of the cooking water into the wok. Add 6 tablespoons of the cooking water and toss until everything is combined and heated through. Serve the noodles topped with the cashews with a few chilli/hot pepper flakes, if you like.

HERO FOOD

AUBERGINE/EGGPLANT

Rich in nasunin, this antioxidant is responsible for the aubergine's glossy, purple skin and has been found to play a protective role in the brain. It is also a good source of fibre, vitamins and minerals.

QUICK IDEAS

SAUCES TO GO . . .

IT´S ALWAYS A GOOD IDEA TO HAVE A GO-TO REPERTOIRE OF SIMPLE, QUICK SAUCES ON STANDBY. THEY CAN HELP TRANSFORM A DISH INTO SOMETHING INTERESTING, TASTY AND SUBSTANTIAL, AS WELL AS BOOSTING ITS NUTRITIONAL VALUE. THESE SAUCES CAN ALSO BE USED AS – OR AS PART OF – A DRESSING OR DIP.

RECIPES SERVE ABOUT 4.

GREAT-FOR-YOU PESTO

This looks like regular basil pesto, but this vibrant green sauce is pimped up with the addition of kale and broccoli – both raw for a maximum vitamin boost.

⇨ Put **2 large handfuls of kale**, tough stalks discarded, **4 broccoli florets**, **1 large garlic clove** and **2 large handfuls of basil leaves** in a food processor and blitz until finely chopped, then tip into a bowl.

⇨ Add **40g/1½oz/heaped ⅓ cup walnuts** to the processor and process until finely chopped, then tip them into a bowl with the veg mixture. Stir in **40g/1½oz/½ cup finely grated Parmesan cheese** and **125ml/4fl oz/ ½ cup extra virgin olive oil** to make a thick sauce, adding extra oil if needed. The pesto will keep for up to 3 days stored in an airtight container in the refrigerator.

ROASTED TOMATO & ALMOND PESTO

For the best-tasting pesto, use vine-ripened tomatoes. Give them a sniff when you buy them – they should smell of tomatoes!

⇨ Preheat the oven to 200°C/400°F/Gas 6. Put **250g/9oz tomatoes** and **3 garlic cloves** in a roasting pan, drizzle **a little olive oil** over the top and toss until everything is coated in the oil. Roast for 30 minutes until the garlic is tender and the tomatoes have started to collapse and colour in places.

▷ Meanwhile, toast **20g/¾oz/2 tablespoons blanched almonds** in a dry frying pan for 4 minutes, turning once, until starting to colour. Put the almonds in a mini food processor and blitz until finely chopped, then tip them into a bowl.

▷ Squeeze the garlic out of its skin and put the cloves in the processor with the roasted tomatoes and **3 tablespoons extra virgin olive oil** and blend until smooth. Tip them into the bowl with the almonds and stir in **20g/¾oz/⅓ cup finely grated pecorino cheese** and stir until combined. The pesto will keep for up to 3 days stored in an airtight container in the refrigerator.

STIR-FRY SAUCE

A vegetable stir-fry makes a great speedy, healthy weekday standby. This simple sauce can be made up to 2 days in advance and kept in the refrigerator until needed. It works well with any combination of vegetables, tofu/beancurd or tempeh.

▷ Simply mix together **2 crushed garlic cloves** and **2.5cm/1in peeled and finely grated fresh root ginger** with **1 tablespoon sesame oil, 2 tablespoons reduced-salt soy sauce** and **6 tablespoons fresh apple juice** (not from concentrate).

▷ Stir-fry your favourite mix of vegetables, enough for 4 people, pour the sauce over and stir-fry for another 2 minutes, adding a splash of water if the sauce is too dry. Serve the stir-fry sprinkled with **toasted nuts** or **seeds**.

FRESH TOMATO SAUCE

Lovely with fritters, savoury pancakes, as a dipping sauce, or spooned over pasta or noodles, this simple fresh tomato sauce takes little time to make.

▷ Put **1–2 tablespoons extra virgin olive oil** in a saucepan with **5 good-size deseeded and chopped vine tomatoes** and heat gently over a medium-low heat for 8 minutes, part-covered with a lid. Add **2 large crushed garlic cloves** and **1 handful of torn basil leaves** or **chopped oregano leaves** and cook for another 2 minutes. Add another drizzle of olive oil and serve warm or at room temperature.

SIMPLE TOMATO SAUCE

Spoon this sauce over pasta, use as a base for a soup or stew, or as a topping on pizza. It makes sense to prepare this stock tomato sauce in large quantities in advance and freeze in ready-to-use portions.

▷ Heat **1 tablespoon olive oil** in a saucepan and add **1 large, finely chopped garlic clove**. Cook for 1 minute before adding **400g/14oz can chopped/crushed tomatoes**, **1 tablespoon tomato purée/paste, 1 teaspoon dried oregano** and **5 tablespoons water**. Bring almost to boiling point, then turn the heat down to low, cover with a lid and simmer for 10 minutes until reduced and thickened, stirring occasionally.

▷ You could stir in **½ teaspoon caster/superfine sugar** to tame the acidity of the tomatoes, if you like. Alternatively, I sometimes stir in **1 tablespoon tomato ketchup** instead of the tomato purée/paste, then there's no need to add the sugar.

THE DOUGH FOR THESE DUMPLINGS IS EASY TO MAKE AND IT´S FUN
TO GET THE KIDS INVOLVED IN THEIR ROLLING AND SHAPING – A STEP
UP FROM PLASTICINE! SERVE WITH THE FRESH TOMATO SAUCE ON
PAGE 101 OR THE ROASTED TOMATO & ALMOND PESTO (SEE PAGE 100)
AND A SALAD OR VEG ON THE SIDE.

RICOTTA DUMPLINGS

Serves 4
Preparation time: 20 minutes
Cooking time: 20 minutes

200g/7oz/scant 1⅔ cups spelt
or plain/all-purpose flour,
plus extra for dusting

½ tsp salt

250g/9oz/heaped 1 cup ricotta
cheese, drained

2 egg yolks

30g/1oz pecorino cheese, finely
grated, plus extra to serve

Fresh Tomato Sauce (see page
101) or Roasted Tomato
& Almond Pesto (see
page 100), to serve

a few basil leaves, chopped,
for sprinkling

1 Mix together the flour and salt in a large mixing bowl.

2 Mix together the ricotta, egg yolks and pecorino in a
separate bowl. Add to the flour mixture and mix together
with a fork and then your hands until combined.

3 Lightly dust a work surface with flour, tip the dumpling
mixture out of the bowl and lightly knead with your hands
for 2 minutes until it forms a soft ball of dough.

4 Divide the dough into 4 pieces. Cover 3 of the pieces with
cling film/plastic wrap and roll out the remaining piece into a
long sausage, about 2cm/¾in diameter. Cut into 1cm/½in long
pieces and put on a floured plate. Repeat with the remaining
pieces of dough.

5 Bring a large pan of water to the boil, add the dumplings
in batches and cook for 3–4 minutes per batch. The dumplings
are ready when they float to the surface. Serve the dumplings
with your choice of sauce and a sprinkling of pecorino and
basil leaves.

HERO FOOD

RICOTTA CHEESE

Dairy foods are a well-known source of the bone- and teeth-
protecting mineral, calcium. What is perhaps lesser known
is the positive effect that milk has on the body after exercise,
including rehydrating, refuelling and repairing – great for
sporty youngsters.

I OFTEN COOK MORE BROWN RICE THAN NEEDED FOR ONE MEAL AS IT MAKES A SUPER-QUICK, HEALTHY ADDITION TO STIR-FRIES, PILAFS, FRITTERS AND SALADS. BEAR IN MIND THAT YOU NEED TO COOL THE COOKED RICE QUICKLY; DO NOT LEAVE IT STANDING AROUND OUT OF THE REFRIGERATOR. IT WILL KEEP FOR UP TO 2 DAYS STORED IN THE REFRIGERATOR AND YOU MUST REHEAT THE RICE UNTIL PIPING HOT.

THAI EGG-FRIED RICE

Serves 4
Preparation time: 15 minutes
Cooking time: 15 minutes

100g/3½oz fine green beans, cut into thirds

1 heaped tbsp coconut oil or sunflower oil

2 tbsp Thai red curry paste

2cm/¾in piece of fresh root ginger, grated (no need to peel)

1 carrot, cut into matchsticks

4 handfuls of edamame beans

1 tbsp reduced-salt soy sauce

600g/1lb 5oz/scant 4½ cups cooked brown basmati rice

4 eggs, lightly beaten

1 handful of chopped coriander/ cilantro leaves (optional)

TO SERVE:

2 spring onions/scallions, finely chopped

1 tbsp toasted sesame seeds

2 handfuls of dry-roasted peanuts, roughly chopped

1 lime, quartered

1 Steam the green beans for 2–3 minutes until lightly cooked and just starting to soften. Refresh under cold running water and leave to drain.

2 Heat the oil in a large wok or frying pan over a medium heat. Add the Thai curry paste and cook, stirring, for 1 minute, then add the ginger, carrot, edamame and green beans and stir-fry for 2 minutes, adding a splash of water if very dry.

3 Add the soy sauce and rice and stir-fry for another 3 minutes until piping hot. Move the rice mixture to one side of the wok and add the eggs. Let the eggs cook, stirring slowly until they start to set in large flakes, then fold the lightly cooked egg into the rice mixture. Stir in the coriander/cilantro, if using.

4 Spoon the rice into four large shallow bowls and top with the spring onions/scallions, sesame seeds and peanuts. Add a squeeze of lime before serving.

HERO FOOD

COCONUT OIL

A good source of energy, coconut oil is rich in lauric acid, which is thought to have antibacterial and antiviral properties. Extra virgin pure coconut oil is best as it is in its purest form.

YOUNG ONES LOVE THE MILD SPICINESS OF MEXICAN FOOD. FOR THESE REFRIED BEANS, I LIKE TO USE A COMBINATION OF BEANS, INCLUDING BORLOTTI, WHICH HAVE A MUCH SOFTER OUTER SKIN THAN KIDNEY BEANS SO ARE EASIER TO BLEND. THEY COME WITH A LIVELY, COLOURFUL CORN SALSA AND ALL-ROUND GOOD-FOR-YOU QUINOA.

MEXICAN REFRIED BEANS
with corn salsa

Serves 4
Preparation time: 15 minutes
Cooking time: 18 minutes

400g/14oz can kidney beans in chilli sauce

400g/14oz can borlotti beans, drained

2 tbsp pumpkin seeds

2 large garlic cloves, peeled and left whole

1 tbsp olive oil

½ –1 tsp chipotle powder or hot smoked paprika (optional)

1 tsp ground cumin

juice and finely grated zest of 1 lime

250g/9oz/1½ cups quinoa

60g/2oz mature/sharp Cheddar cheese, grated

Blackened Corn Salsa (see page 133) and crisp salad, to serve

1 Put the kidney beans and their sauce, half the borlotti beans, the pumpkin seeds and garlic in a blender and blend to a coarse paste.

2 Spoon the bean mixture into a frying pan with the oil, the remaining borlotti beans, the chipotle powder, cumin and lime juice. Heat over a medium-low heat for 8 minutes, stirring often, until reduced and thickened. Stir in the lime zest.

3 Meanwhile, cook the quinoa, following the instructions on the packet, until tender. Drain.

4 To serve, spoon the quinoa onto serving plates, top with the beans, cheese and then the corn salsa, with a salad on the side.

HERO FOOD

GARLIC
Praised for its health-giving properties for centuries, garlic is reputed to be antiviral, antibacterial and antifungal.

GRIDDLING THE CORN FIRST ADDS A LOVELY SMOKINESS TO THESE FRITTERS – THIS ISN'T ESSENTIAL BUT IF TIME ALLOWS IT'S WORTH THE EFFORT. IF YOU DON'T HAVE GRAM/CHICKPEA FLOUR, DO SWAP IT FOR SPELT OR PLAIN/ALL-PURPOSE FLOUR. YOU COULD ALSO SERVE THE CORN CAKES IN A BUN WITH YOUR FAVOURITE ACCOMPANIMENTS.

CORN CAKES
with avocado mayo

Serves 4
Preparation time: 20 minutes
Cooking time: 18 minutes

3 corn-on-the-cobs, husks removed

1 tsp olive oil, plus extra for frying

200g/7oz/1½ cups cooked brown rice

4 spring onions/scallions, chopped

1 egg

1 tsp ground cumin

1 tsp ground coriander

1 large pinch of dried chilli/hot pepper flakes (optional)

3 tbsp gram/chickpea flour, plus extra for dusting

roasted tomatoes and Crispy Courgette Sticks (see page 133), to serve

AVOCADO MAYO:

2 avocadoes, halved, pitted and peeled

1 large garlic clove, crushed

juice of 1 lime

4 tbsp mayonnaise

1 Place a griddle pan over a high heat. Brush the corn cobs with oil and cook for 10 minutes, turning regularly, until they start to blacken in places, then leave to cool. Stand one of the cobs on its end and carefully slice off the kernels, then repeat with the remaining cobs.

2 Put two-thirds of the corn kernels in a food processor with the rice, spring onions/scallions, egg, spices and gram/chickpea flour and whiz to a coarse paste. Stir in the remaining corn kernels.

3 Generously dust a plate and your hands with flour and form the corn mixture into 4 patties. (The mixture is quite loose, so would benefit from 15 minutes or so in the freezer to firm up.)

4 Meanwhile, make the avocado mayo. Mash the avocado in a bowl until almost smooth and mix in the rest of the ingredients. Taste and add a splash more lime juice, if needed.

5 Generously coat the bottom of a large frying pan with oil and cook the corn cakes over a medium heat for 3–4 minutes on each side until golden. Serve with the avocado mayo, roasted tomatoes and the crispy courgette sticks.

GRAM FLOUR

Made from ground chickpeas, gram flour is gluten-free and is a good source of protein, fibre, B vitamins, iron, selenium, magnesium and manganese.

NOT ONLY IS TURMERIC A WONDER SPICE HEALTHWISE, IT ALSO MAKES
EVERYTHING LOOK SO SUNNY AND INVITING. I PREFER TO USE BROWN
BASMATI RICE AS IT HAS A LOVELY NUTTY FLAVOUR AND KEEPS ITS
TEXTURE WHEN COOKED, PLUS, MOST IMPORTANTLY, IT RETAINS
VALUABLE NUTRIENTS AND FIBRE WHEN UNREFINED. I FIND THE KIDS
DON'T SEEM TO NOTICE WHEN IT'S COLOURED WITH TURMERIC, TOO.

YELLOW RICE PILAF

Serves 4
Preparation time: 15 minutes
Cooking time: 30 minutes

30g/1oz/2 tbsp butter

1 large onion, roughly chopped

2 handfuls of blanched almonds

2 tbsp mild curry powder

250g/9oz/scant 1⅓ cups brown
   basmati rice

2.5cm/1in piece of fresh root
   ginger, grated (no need to peel)

1 tsp turmeric

600ml/21fl oz/2½ cups reduced-
   salt vegetable stock

2 handfuls of frozen peas

½ cauliflower, cut into florets,
   grated

1 handful of parsley, chopped
   (optional)

1 tbsp olive oil

LEMON YOGURT:

150g/5½oz/scant ⅔ cup
   Greek yogurt

1 small garlic clove, crushed

2 tbsp lemon juice

finely grated zest of ½ lemon

1 Melt the butter in a saucepan over a medium-low heat.
Add the onion and cook for 10 minutes, covered with a lid and
stirring occasionally, until softened.

2 While the onion is cooking, toss the almonds in half of the
curry powder and leave to one side.

3 Mix together all the ingredients for the lemon yogurt in
a bowl and leave to one side.

4 When the onions are cooked, add the rice, ginger, the
remaining curry powder, the turmeric and the stock (the rice
should be covered by about 1cm/½in stock). Bring to the boil,
then turn the heat down to its lowest setting, cover with a lid
and cook for 20 minutes.

5 Stir the peas into the rice, quickly cover with a lid and cook
for another 5 minutes, or until the water has been absorbed
and the rice is tender. Stir the cauliflower and parsley into the
rice until combined, cover with a lid and leave to stand on the
turned-off hob/stovetop.

6 While the rice is cooking, heat the oil in a large frying
pan over a medium heat. Add the spice-coated almonds and
cook for about 4 minutes, shaking occasionally, until they
smell aromatic and toasted. Serve the yellow rice with a good
spoonful of the lemon yogurt and topped with the spiced nuts.

MORE OFTEN THAN NOT THE RECIPES YOU PUT OFF TESTING TURN OUT
TO BE THE BEST AND THIS IS ONE OF THEM. I'M NOT SURE WHY I WAS
SO RELUCTANT, BUT THIS MILDLY SPICED CURRY TURNED OUT TO BE A
REAL WINNER. THE CASHEWS BOOST THE NUTRITIONAL VALUE AS WELL
AS GIVING A THICK CREAMINESS TO THE SAUCE AND THE HALLOUMI
DEVELOPS A WONDERFUL SOFT TEXTURE WHEN COOKED IN THE SAUCE.

CHEESY-PEAS CASHEW KORMA

Serves 4
Preparation time: 10 minutes
Cooking time: 20 minutes

80g/2¾oz/⅔ cup cashew nuts
1 heaped tbsp coconut oil
1 large onion, chopped
3 garlic cloves, chopped
4cm/1½in piece of fresh root
    ginger, peeled and coarsely
    grated
2 tbsp garam masala
1 tsp turmeric
125g/4½oz/1 cup frozen peas
225g/8oz halloumi, cut into
    1cm/½in cubes
6 tbsp coconut drinking milk
juice of 1 lime
2 tbsp chopped coriander/cilantro
    leaves (optional)
freshly ground black pepper
brown basmati rice, to serve

1 Put the cashews in a large, dry frying pan over a medium heat and toast for 5 minutes, turning occasionally, until light golden. Tip into a mini food processor with 100ml/3½fl oz/ scant ½ cup water and blend until smooth and creamy.

2 Meanwhile, heat the coconut oil in a saucepan over a medium heat. Add the onion and cook, covered with a lid, for 5 minutes until softened but not coloured. Stir the onion occasionally to stop it sticking. Add the garlic and ginger and cook, stirring, for another minute.

3 Put the onion mixture in a mini food processor with 100ml/3½fl oz/½ cup water and blend until smooth, then return it to the pan with the cashew nut mixture.

4 Stir in the spices, peas, halloumi, coconut milk and 125ml/ 4fl oz/½ cup water and bring almost to the boil, then turn the heat down, cover and simmer for 8–10 minutes until the peas are tender. Stir in the lime juice and coriander/cilantro, if using, and season with pepper. Serve the curry with rice.

CASHEW NUTS
Rich in vitamins B and E, magnesium, calcium and iron, nuts provide an abundance of beneficial nutrients to a meat-free diet.

SPROUTING SEEDS

NOTE TO ADULT HELPERS:

Getting kids involved in growing their own fresh food is both educational and fun. It's a great way of teaching them where fruit and veg come from, how they grow, what varieties look like and, in my experience, encourages them to try what they grow. It certainly got my son into eating salad!

You don't need a large garden to grow your own fresh veg or herbs; a few pots or even a reused can with holes punctured in the base make ideal containers. We successfully grew pea shoots and cress in a can.

Seeds are cheap to buy and a pack will provide bountiful amounts of produce. Start with the easy-to-grow varieties such as radishes, salad leaves, spring onions/scallions, bush beans, rocket/arugula and other herbs, which will all flourish in a pot of potting compost if it's watered regularly.

You could start your child off by sprouting seeds, which can be done at any time of the year and doesn't require any special equipment. Alfalfa are perhaps the easiest and have long, spindly shoots, topped with small green leaves and a peppery flavour.

HOW TO SPROUT ALFALFA

2 tbsp organic alfalfa seeds
1 large jam/conserve jar
piece of muslin/cheesecloth large enough
   to fit over the top of the jar with surplus
rubber band

⇨ Wash your hands well. Rinse the alfalfa seeds well in a sieve/fine-mesh strainer under cold running water.

⇨ Tip the seeds into a large jam/conserve jar and pour in enough cool water to cover.

⇨ Place a piece of muslin/cheescloth over the top of the jar, secure it with a rubber band and leave the jar to stand overnight.

⇨ Next day, drain away the water through the muslin/cheesecloth and cover again with cool water. Gently shake the jar, then pour the water out.

⟴ Leave the jar on its side, so that the air can circulate, and place it in a draught free place away from direct sunlight.

⟴ For the next few days, rinse the seeds in the morning and in the evening by filling the jar with some water, gently swishing the seeds around and then draining. The seeds should have sprouted by day 3–5.

⟴ The alfalfa sprouts are now ready to eat. Store them in a container covered with a lid in the refrigerator. They will keep for 2–3 days.

SPROUTS CAN BE SUBJECT TO
- -
CONTAMINATION. BUY ORGANIC
- -
SPROUTS OR, IF SPROUTING AT
- -
HOME, CLEAN YOUR HANDS AND
- -
ALL EQUIPMENT WELL. STORE
- -
SPROUTS IN THE REFRIGERATOR
- -
AND EAT WITHIN 2-3 DAYS.
- -

WEEKENDS

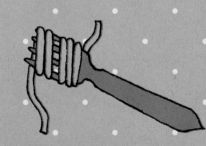

← LEFT, SPEEDY PAN PIZZAS. RECIPE ON PAGE 140.

EVERYONE LOVES DUMPLINGS . . . SO WHY NOT GET THE KIDS INVOLVED IN MAKING THEM? THESE CHINESE DUMPLINGS – OR POTSTICKERS AS THEY ARE ALSO KNOWN – AREN´T PARTICULARLY FIDDLY, BUT LOTS OF HANDS MAKE LIGHT WORK. FILLED WITH TOFU/BEANCURD, PAK CHOI/ BOK CHOY AND SPRING ONIONS/SCALLIONS, OTHER GOOD FILLINGS ARE GRATED RAW CARROT, ASPARAGUS AND CABBAGE.

POTSTICKERS

Makes 24
Preparation time: 20 minutes
(less with help!)
Cooking time: 10 minutes

24 round gyoza or wonton
  wrappers
2 tbsp sunflower oil
snipped chives, for sprinkling

TOFU FILLING:

175g/6oz tofu/beancurd, drained
  well, patted dry and coarsely
  grated
1 pak choi/bok choy, very finely
  chopped
3 spring onions/scallions, finely
  chopped
2.5cm/1in piece of fresh root
  ginger, peeled and grated
1 tbsp reduced-salt soy sauce
1 tsp sesame oil

SOY DIPPING SAUCE:

3 tbsp reduced-salt soy sauce
1 tbsp sesame oil
1 tbsp toasted sesame seeds
sprinkling of dried chilli/hot
  pepper flakes (optional)

1 Mix together the ingredients for the filling in a bowl.

2 Mix together the ingredients for the dipping sauce, adding the chilli/hot pepper flakes, if you like.

3 To assemble the dumplings, place a heaped teaspoon of the filling mixture in the middle of a gyoza or wonton wrapper. Dip your finger into a bowl of water and use your damp finger to dampen the edge of the wrapper. Fold the wrapper in half and press the edges together, crimping them as you go to make a half-moon-shaped dumpling.

4 Lightly press the dumpling on a work surface to flatten the bottom. Put it on a plate and cover with a clean, damp dish towel. Repeat to make 24 dumplings in total.

5 Heat half the oil over a medium heat in a large frying pan with a lid. Arrange half the dumplings in the pan, flat-side down, and cook for 2 minutes, or until the base is golden and slightly crisp. Add 5 tablespoons water to the pan, cover with a lid and simmer for 2 minutes, or until most of the liquid is absorbed. Transfer the cooked dumplings to a warm plate and cover with cling film/plastic wrap to keep warm while you cook the remaining dumplings.

6 To serve, sprinkle the dumplings with chives and tuck in, dipping the potstickers in the dipping sauce.

HERO FOOD

GINGER
Fresh ginger is brilliant for supporting the digestive system and soothing stomach cramps and nausea.

I LIKE TO USE RED QUINOA TO MAKE THESE SUBSTANTIAL BURGERS FOR ITS COLOUR AND NUTTY TEXTURE, BUT ANY VARIETY WILL DO. LIKEWISE, DO TRY OTHER TYPES OF BEANS – MAYBE KIDNEY BEANS, BLACK BEANS OR BUTTER/LIMA BEANS. IF YOU WANT TO USE DRIED BEANS, FACTOR IN EXTRA TIME FOR SOAKING AND PRE-COOKING – YOU'LL NEED ABOUT 115G/4OZ/HEAPED ½ CUP.

QUINOA & HALLOUMI BURGERS
with corn salsa

118

Serves 4
Preparation time: 20 minutes,
    plus chilling
Cooking time: 40 minutes

55g/2oz/¼ cup red quinoa
400g/14oz can borlotti beans,
    drained and rinsed
1 small onion, grated
2 garlic cloves, finely chopped
2 tsp dried thyme
175g/6oz halloumi, patted dry
    and grated
1 egg, lightly beaten
flour, for dusting
Blackened Corn Salsa
    (see page 133)
sunflower oil, for frying

TO SERVE:

4 soft seeded buns, preferably
    wholegrain, split in half
2 tbsp mayonnaise
4 crisp lettuce leaves
2 tomatoes, sliced

1 Put the quinoa in a saucepan, cover with water and bring to the boil. Cover with a lid and simmer over a medium-low heat for 15–18 minutes until tender, then drain well and cool.

2 Put the quinoa and borlotti beans in a mixing bowl and roughly mash using a potato masher. Add the onion, garlic, thyme, halloumi and egg, then stir until combined.

3 Coat a plate and your hands with flour. Shape the bean mixture into 4 burgers and dust each one with flour. Place the burgers on a plate and chill for 20 minutes to firm up.

4 Meanwhile, to make the salsa turn to page 133. Blend half of the chargrilled corn to a coarse paste. Transfer the corn paste to a bowl and stir in the rest of the corn with the remaining ingredients, adding the chillies, if you like. Leave the salsa to one side.

5 Pour enough oil to generously cover the bottom of a large frying pan and heat over a medium heat. Add the burgers and fry for 6–8 minutes, turning once, until golden and crisp.

6 To assemble the burgers, lightly toast the buns. Spread the mayonnaise over one side of each bun and top with the lettuce, burgers, tomatoes and a good spoonful of the corn salsa. Top with the bun lid and serve.

QUINOA

Pronounced ´keen-wa´, this gluten-free grain is a complete protein, meaning it provides all the amino acids necessary for the repair and maintenance of the body´s cells, tissues and muscles.

A BIG POT OF CHILLI IS A GREAT WAY TO FEED A CROWD AND THIS ONE IS HEAVING WITH FLAVOUR AND GOODNESS – AND COMES WITH AN ADDED SECRET INGREDIENT! THE CHIPOTLE CHILLI ADDS A BURST OF HEAT, BUT IF YOU'RE LOOKING FOR SOMETHING A BIT TAMER, JUST STICK TO MILD SMOKED PAPRIKA. SERVE THE CHILLI WITH BROWN RICE AND EXTRAS SUCH AS CRISP TORTILLAS, GUACAMOLE AND CHEESE.

BIG VEG CHILLI

Serves 6–8
Preparation time: 20 minutes
Cooking time: 40 minutes

2 tbsp olive oil

1 large onion, finely chopped

1 carrot, finely chopped

1 red pepper, deseeded and finely chopped

3 garlic cloves, finely chopped

1 tsp chipotle powder (or use extra smoked paprika)

1 tsp ground allspice or cinnamon

2 tsp sweet mild smoked paprika

2 x 400g/14oz cans chopped/crushed tomatoes

1 tbsp tomato purée/paste

400g/14oz can green lentils, drained

400g/14oz can kidney beans, drained

2 tsp yeast extract

2 cooked beetroot/beets, sliced

140g/5oz/1 cup sweetcorn kernels

freshly ground black pepper

See introduction, above, for serving suggestions

1 Heat the oil in a large casserole over a medium heat. Add the onion, carrot and red pepper and cook for 10 minutes, stirring often, until softened.

2 Add the garlic, spices, tomatoes, tomato purée/paste, lentils, beans, yeast extract and 125ml/4fl oz/½ cup water. Stir well, bring to the boil, then turn the heat down to medium-low and simmer, part-covered with a lid, for 20 minutes until the sauce has reduced and thickened.

3 While the chilli is cooking, purée the beetroot/beets with a stick/immersion blender. Stir the beetroot/beets and corn into the chilli and cook for another 5–10 minutes, adding a splash more water if the sauce is too thick.

4 Serve in bowls with rice topped with guacamole and grated cheese and crisp tortillas by the side.

HERO FOOD

LENTILS
High in fibre and low in fat, lentils provide a wide range of vitamins and minerals, including iron, calcium, zinc, potassium and some B vitamins.

THIS CAJUN-INSPIRED RICE DISH IS EASY TO MAKE AND MAKES A PERFECT WEEKEND LUNCH OR EVEN BRUNCH. IT COMES TOPPED WITH A POACHED EGG AND A PEA GUACAMOLE, BUT DO TRY OTHER TOPPINGS. I ALSO LIKE THE RICE WITH A SPOONFUL OF HOUMOUS OR SOUR CREAM, OR CHOPPED ROASTED PEANUTS AND THICK YOGURT, OR GRATED CHEESE AND A SPLASH OF SRIRACHA.

CAJUN RICE BOWL

Serves 4
Preparation time: 20 minutes
Cooking time: 40 minutes

1 tbsp olive oil

1 large onion, chopped

1 carrot, grated

3 garlic cloves, finely chopped

2.5cm/1in piece of fresh root ginger, grated (no need to peel)

1 tbsp Cajun spice mix

1 heaped tsp turmeric

250g/9oz/scant 1⅓ cups brown basmati rice

600ml/21fl oz/2½ cups reduced-salt vegetable stock

30g/1oz/2 tbsp butter

4 large eggs

Pea Guacamole (see page 47) and 1 lime, cut into wedges, to serve

1 Heat the oil in a saucepan over a medium heat. Add the onion and carrot, cover with a lid and sauté for 8 minutes, stirring occasionally, until softened. Mix in the garlic, ginger, spice mix, turmeric and rice.

2 Pour in the stock, bring to the boil, then turn the heat down to its lowest setting, cover and simmer for 25 minutes, or until the stock has been absorbed and the rice is tender. Stir in the butter, then cover and leave the rice to stand for 5 minutes.

3 To poach the eggs, heat a deep sauté pan of water to just below boiling point. Turn the heat down to low, swirl the water and crack the eggs, one at a time, into the pan. Poach the eggs in the gently simmering water for a few minutes until the whites set but the yolks remains runny.

4 Spoon the rice into bowls, top with the eggs and a good spoonful of pea guacamole and serve with extra lime wedges.

HERO FOOD

BROWN RICE

In terms of nutrients, brown rice wins hands down over white. Along with fibre, it provides beneficial amounts of vitamins and minerals, including manganese for a healthy nervous system.

A PACK OF PUFF PASTRY ALWAYS MAKES A USEFUL STANDBY AND CAN BE TRANSFORMED INTO ALL SORTS OF SWEET AND SAVOURY GOODIES. FOR INSTANCE, IMPRESS FRIENDS AND FAMILY WITH THIS ROAST VEGETABLE TART WITH A PUFF PASTRY BASE. IT PUFFS UP MAJESTICALLY DURING BAKING AND LOOKS MUCH HARDER TO MAKE THAN IT ACTUALLY IS.

ROAST VEGGIE TART

Serves 4
Preparation time: 20 minutes
Cooking time: 40 minutes

2 tbsp olive oil, plus extra for greasing

1 red pepper, deseeded and cut into long slices

1 yellow pepper, deseeded and cut into long slices

2 onions, each cut into 8 wedges

1 courgette/zucchini, cut into long slices

320g/11¼oz ready-rolled sheet puff pastry

1 egg, lightly beaten

200g/7oz sundried tomato pesto

4 tbsp cream cheese

2 tbsp toasted pine nuts

30g/1oz Parmesan cheese, grated into shavings

1 handful of basil leaves (optional)

1   Preheat the oven to 200°C/400°F/Gas 6. Lightly oil a large baking sheet.

2   Put all the vegetables in a large bowl, pour in the oil and turn to coat them in the oil. Spread the vegetables out onto another two large baking sheets and roast for 30–40 minutes until tender and golden in places.

3   Meanwhile, unroll the pastry and place on the prepared baking sheet. Fold in the edges of the pastry to make a raised border and brush all over with egg. Bake in the top of the oven (above the vegetables) for 25 minutes until almost cooked.

4   Remove the pastry from the oven. Turn the vegetables and swap the sheets round. Spoon the pesto over the top of the pastry and return it to the oven for another 5–8 minutes until risen and golden and the base is cooked and crisp.

5   To assemble, arrange the roasted vegetables on top of the tart and add spoonfuls of the cream cheese. Scatter over the pine nuts, Parmesan and basil, if using, before serving.

ONIONS
Antibacterial and antiviral, onions are also a good source of antioxidants.

I COULDN'T RESIST ADDING A FEW SPICES TO THIS HEARTY VEGGIE
VERSION OF SHEPHERD'S PIE, BUT FOR A MORE CLASSIC FLAVOURING
OPT FOR HERBS INSTEAD – THYME, ROSEMARY AND PARSLEY WOULD
ALL WORK. THE SAUCE CAN BE MADE IN ADVANCE AND WILL HAPPILY
SIT FOR A COUPLE OF DAYS IN THE REFRIGERATOR.

INDIAN VEG PIE

Serves 6–8
Preparation time: 20 minutes
Cooking time: 1 hour

2 tbsp olive oil
2 onions, finely chopped
1 celery stalk, thinly sliced
2 carrots, diced
2 parsnips, diced
5 garlic cloves, peeled and left
    whole
200g/7oz/heaped 1 cup green
    lentils
2.5cm/1in piece of fresh root
    ginger, peeled and grated
1½–2 tbsp mild curry powder
1 tsp turmeric
400g/14oz can chopped/crushed
    tomatoes
1 vegetable stock/bouillon cube
2 heaped tbsp tomato purée/
    paste
freshly ground black pepper

SWEET POTATO TOPPING:
4–5 large sweet potatoes, peeled
    and cut into large chunks
30g/1oz/2 tbsp butter
100g/3½oz mature/sharp
    Cheddar cheese, grated

1 Heat the oil in a large flameproof casserole over a medium heat. Add the onions, celery, carrots and parsnips and cook, covered and stirring occasionally, for 8 minutes until softened.

2 Chop 3 of the garlic cloves and stir into the casserole with the lentils, ginger and spices. Pour in the tomatoes, then fill the can with water and add to the pan, then add a second can of water. Bring to the boil, crumble in the stock/bouillon cube and add the tomato purée/paste. Stir, part-cover with a lid and simmer for 20–25 minutes, or until the lentils are cooked.

3 Meanwhile, preheat the oven to 220°C/425°F/Gas 7. To make the topping, boil the sweet potatoes with the remaining garlic cloves for 10 minutes, or until tender. Drain the potatoes and return them to the pan to dry on the turned off hob/stovetop. Add the butter and half the cheese and mash until smooth.

4 Season the sauce with pepper and check the flavouring, adding more curry powder, if needed. Using a stick/immersion blender, partially purée the sauce – you want a combination of chunky and smooth and not too liquid. If the sauce is too runny, cook it without the lid until reduced down.

5 Spoon the mashed potatoes on top of the sauce (or spoon the sauce into one large or individual ovenproof dishes and top with the mash). Scatter the remaining cheese over and bake for 20–25 minutes until the top is crisp and golden.

HERO FOOD

PARSNIPS

A great way to add fibre to your diet, parsnips also contain vitamin C, folate and potassium, which promote a healthy nervous system.

LOVE IT OR HATE IT, IF YOU COAT TOFU/BEANCURD IN A CRISP
BATTER YOU ARE SURE TO WIN OVER ANY DISSENTERS. THIS VEGGIE
ALTERNATIVE TO A BRITISH CLASSIC COMES WITH SWEET POTATO
FRIES AND MINTY CRUSHED PEAS. THE TOFU/BEANCURD IS ALSO
GOOD SERVED ASIAN-STYLE WITH A STIR-FRY AND RICE OR NOODLES.

CRISPY BATTERED TOFU, CHIPS <u>AND</u> MINTY PEAS

Serves 4
Preparation time: 15 minutes
Cooking time: 20 minutes

sunflower oil, for frying, plus
extra for the peas
600g/1lb 5oz tofu/beancurd,
drained well, patted dry and
cut into 12 x 1cm/½in-thick
slices
80g/2¾oz/¾ cup cornflour/
cornstarch
2 eggs
Spicy Sweet Potato Fries,
omitting the spices if
preferred (see page 133),
to serve

MINTY PEAS:
300g/10½oz/2¼ cups frozen
peas
1 large handful of mint leaves,
finely chopped

1 First, make the minty peas. Cover the peas with water in
a pan, bring to the boil and cook for 3 minutes until tender.
Drain, reserving 4 tablespoons of the cooking water. Return
the peas to the pan with the water and a splash of oil. Stir in
the mint, then crush with a potato masher to a coarse purée.
Cover and leave to one side.

2 Meanwhile, drain the slices of tofu on a double-layered
sheet of paper towels – it's vital to get rid of as much water as
possible. Put the cornflour/cornstarch in a large shallow bowl.

3 Lightly beat the eggs in a separate large shallow bowl.

4 To prepare the tofu, pour enough oil into a large sauté pan
so that it is about 1cm/½in deep and heat over a medium heat.
Test it is ready by frying a small piece of bread, which should
become golden and crisp in about 45 seconds.

5 Dunk a slice of the tofu into the cornflour/cornstarch
until evenly and thoroughly coated, then dip it into the egg.
Carefully place the tofu in the hot oil and repeat with 3 more
slices. Cook for about 5 minutes, turning once, until golden
and crisp all over. Drain on paper towels and keep warm in
a low oven while you repeat with the remaining tofu.

6 Just before serving, briefly warm the peas, if necessary, and
served topped with the tofu and sweet potato fries on the side.

PEAS

You'll always find a bag of peas in my freezer. Not only are they super-convenient, they provide a bundle of nutrients, such as vitamins A, C, K and many of the Bs. Since peas are frozen straight after picking, these nutrients are found in beneficial amounts.

WHO WOULD HAVE THOUGHT THAT CAULIFLOWER MAKES A GREAT, HEALTHY BASE FOR PIZZA? AS A DOUBLE WHAMMY, IT WENT DOWN REALLY WELL WITH MY BOY. THE COMBINATION OF CAULI, OATS, QUINOA FLAKES AND ALMONDS MAKES A CRISP, NUTTY CRUST. I'VE OPTED FOR A SIMPLE VEGETABLE TOPPING, BUT DO GO WITH YOUR OWN FAVOURITES.

CAULI PIZZA

Serves 2–4
Preparation time: 10 minutes,
plus chilling
Cooking time: 40 minutes

CAULIFLOWER CRUST:

1 cauliflower, outer leaves
and main stalk removed,
cut into florets

50g/1¾oz/heaped ½ cup oats

40g/1½oz/heaped ⅓ cup quinoa
flakes (or use just oats)

100g/3½oz/1 cup ground almonds

2 tbsp nutritional yeast flakes

2 eggs, lightly beaten

extra virgin olive oil, for greasing
and drizzling

TOPPING:

½ recipe quantity Simple Tomato
Sauce (see page 101)

1 small red onion, sliced into
rings

6 mushrooms, sliced

150g/5½oz mozzarella cheese,
drained, patted dry and torn
into chunks

1 handful of basil and/or rocket/
arugula leaves

1 To make the crust, put the cauliflower florets in a food processor, blitz to fine grains, then tip them into a bowl. Put the oats and quinoa in the processor and blitz until coarsely ground. Add them to the bowl with the cauliflower and mix in the remaining ingredients. Use your hands to press the mixture into a coarse, slightly wet, flat round of 'dough'. Wrap the dough and chill for 30 minutes to firm up slightly.

2 Preheat the oven to 220°C/425°F/Gas 7. Line a large baking sheet with baking parchment and grease generously with oil.

3 Put the dough on the prepared baking sheet and press it out with your fingers to a thin, even crust, about 1cm/½in thick, and with a slightly thicker raised edge. Bake for 25 minutes, or until crisp and slightly golden around the edges.

4 When the crust is ready, smear the tomato sauce over the top, leaving a border. Top with the onion, mushrooms and mozzarella. Drizzle a little extra olive oil over and bake for 10–15 minutes until the mozzarella has melted. Cut the pizza into wedges and scatter the basil and rocket/arugula leaves over, if using, before serving.

CAULIFLOWER

Choline is just one of the many nutrients found in cauliflower, which has been found to help with memory and learning.

THESE MUSHROOMS MAKE A GREAT VEGGIE ADDITION TO A SUMMER BARBECUE. MARINATED IN A STICKY BARBECUE SAUCE – ALWAYS A WINNER WITH KIDS – THEY COME TOPPED WITH HALLOUMI AND A RED PEPPER HOUMOUS, ALTHOUGH CHILLI SAUCE MIXED INTO MAYO IS ALSO GOOD. YOU DON´T NEED A FLASHY BARBECUE TO COOK THEM, A DISPOSABLE ONE WILL DO, OR GRIDDLE THEM INSTEAD.

STICKY BBQ MUSHROOMS

Serves 4
Preparation time: 20 minutes,
plus marinating
Cooking time: 20 minutes

4 large flat mushrooms,
   stalks removed
250g/9oz halloumi, cut into
   8 thick slices
Red Pepper Houmous
   (see page 46)
4 wholegrain seeded buns,
   split and lightly toasted
pea shoots, slices of tomato
   and Alfalfa Sprouts (see
   page 112), to serve

BARBECUE SAUCE:

3 tbsp tomato ketchup
2 tbsp reduced-salt soy sauce
1 tbsp clear honey
1 tbsp balsamic vinegar
1 tbsp olive oil, plus extra
   for cooking

1 Mix together all the ingredients for the barbecue sauce. Place the mushrooms in a large dish and spoon the barbecue sauce over to coat both sides. Marinate for about 1 hour. (You can cook them straightaway, if time is tight.)

2 Brush the barbecue or griddle with a little oil. Add the mushrooms and cook for 15 minutes, turning once and pressing them down once they have started to soften, until tender and they've blackened slightly.

3 Put the mushrooms in a dish and cover with foil to keep warm. If using a griddle, wipe it after cooking the mushrooms. Brush both sides of the halloumi with oil and barbecue or griddle for 3 minutes, turning once, until charred in places.

4 Spread the houmous on one half of each bun and top with a few pea shoots, followed by the mushrooms, halloumi, tomato and alfalfa. Top with the bun lids and serve straightaway.

HERO FOOD

MUSHROOMS

Mushrooms are a good source of energy-boosting B vitamins, and are also reputed to help support the immune system.

HERO
FOOD

LEEKS
An excellent source of vitamin K,
this nutrient is needed for blood
clotting and bone health.

THE HOURS CAN WHIZ BY WHEN TESTING RECIPES, AS MY POOR FAMILY WILL CONFIRM HAVING HAD TO WAIT TO EAT ON MANY AN OCCASION. HAPPILY, THIS WAS A RECIPE THAT WAS WORTH WAITING FOR – IT GOT A UNIVERSAL THUMBS UP. THE INDIVIDUAL PIES HAVE A COBBLER TOPPING AND A CREAMY MUSHROOM AND LEEK FILLING.

PIE IN A MUG

Serves 4
Preparation time: 20 minutes,
**   plus soaking**
Cooking time: 50 minutes

15g/½oz dried porcini
30g/1oz/2 tbsp butter
1 tbsp olive oil
1 large onion, chopped
2 large leeks, chopped
250g/9oz mushrooms, chopped
2 large garlic cloves, chopped
1 tsp dried thyme
1 heaped tbsp spelt flour
100g/3½oz cream cheese
100ml/3½fl oz/scant ½ cup milk
freshly ground black pepper

COBBLER TOPPING:

175g/6oz/scant 1½ cups spelt
    flour
60g/2¼oz/heaped ⅓ cup
    wholegrain spelt flour
2 tsp baking powder
½ tsp salt
100g/3½oz/7 tbsp chilled butter,
    cubed
2 tbsp nutritional yeast flakes
100ml/3½fl oz/scant ½ cup
    buttermilk
1 egg, lightly beaten, to glaze

1 Put the dried porcini in a small bowl and cover with 100ml/3½fl oz/scant ½ cup just-boiled water. Leave to soften for 20 minutes while you prepare the cobbler topping.

2 Put the flours, baking powder and salt in a mixing bowl. Using your fingertips, lightly rub the butter into the flour mixture until it resembles fine breadcrumbs. Stir in the yeast flakes and buttermilk and bring the mixture together into a soft ball of dough. Add more buttermilk or flour, if needed. Wrap in cling film/plastic wrap and chill until ready to use.

3 Preheat the oven to 200°C/400°F/Gas 6. Heat the butter and oil in a pan and sauté the onion and leeks until softened.

4 Drain the porcini, reserving the soaking water. Finely chop the porcini and add them to the pan with the mushrooms, garlic and thyme. Cook for another 5 minutes until softened and most of the liquid has evaporated. Add the flour and cook, stirring, for 2 minutes. Add the porcini soaking liquid, cream cheese and milk and season with black pepper. Stir and cook for 5 minutes until thickened.

5 Spoon the mushroom mixture into four large ovenproof mugs or a dish. Quarter the cobbler dough and form into rounds 2cm/¾in thick to fit snuggly on top of each mug. Brush the tops with egg. Put the mugs in a roasting pan and bake for 25–30 minutes until the pies have risen and are cooked through. Leave for a few minutes to cool slightly before serving in the mugs or decanting onto plates.

QUICK IDEAS

ON THE SIDE...

IT'S EASY TO FOCUS ON THE MAIN PART OF A MEAL BUT IT'S THE ADDED EXTRAS THAT CAN MAKE ALL THE DIFFERENCE. A GRAVY OR SAUCE IS PERFECT FOR UNIFYING ALL THE VARIOUS PARTS OF A MEAL AS WELL AS GIVING YOU THE OPPORTUNITY TO BOOST ITS NUTRITIONAL CONTENT.

WHEN IT COMES TO SIDE VEG, I'M AS GUILTY AS MOST FOR SIMPLY STEAMING SOME BROCCOLI OR BOILING A PAN OF PEAS. BUT BY ADDING EXTRA FLAVOURINGS OR USING DIFFERENT METHODS OF COOKING YOU CAN REALLY BUMP UP THE FLAVOUR OF VEGGIES AND HOPEFULLY INCREASE THEIR APPEAL.

RECIPES SERVE ABOUT 4.

EASY ONION GRAVY

A must with veggie sausages, pies and roasts or use as a base for a stew or soup.

➾ Melt **20g/¾oz/1½ tbsp butter** in a saucepan over a medium-low heat, then add **2 sliced onions** and cook, stirring, for 10 minutes until softened and golden. Stir in **4 teaspoons spelt** or **plain/all-purpose flour** and keep stirring for 2 minutes until the flour starts to colour.

➾ Gradually add **455ml/16fl oz/scant 2 cups hot reduced-salt vegetable stock**, stirring continuously. Add **1 teaspoon yeast extract** and **1 tablespoon reduced-salt soy sauce** and let the gravy gently bubble away for 8–10 minutes until reduced and thickened, stirring occasionally.

TAHINI-MISO DRESSING

Spooned over roasted vegetables, salads or grains, this creamy dressing adds extra interest to all sorts of side dishes.

➾ Mix together **2 tablespoons tahini sauce** with **1 tablespoon white miso**, **1 teaspoon clear honey** and **1 finely chopped garlic clove**. Stir in **2 tablespoons warm water** until smooth and creamy.

SPICY SWEET POTATO FRIES

These make a great alternative to regular chips/fries and oven wedges.

⊳ Preheat the oven to 200°C/400°F/Gas 6. Slice **4 scrubbed sweet potatoes** into wedges and toss in **2 tablespoons olive oil** or **melted coconut oil**.

⊳ Sprinkle **2 teaspoons of your favourite spice mix** over the potatoes – it could be Indian, Thai, Cajun, Mexican or Moroccan – and spread them out in an even layer on one or two large baking sheets. Roast for 30–40 minutes, turning once, until cooked, golden and crisp.

CRISPY COURGETTE STICKS

A coating of ground almonds and Parmesan cheese gives even the most ordinary vegetables extra pizzazz.

⊳ Preheat the oven to 200°C/400°F/Gas 6 and oil two baking sheets. Cut **4 courgettes/zucchini** in half and then each half into batons or wedges – don´t slice them too thinly.

⊳ Brush the courgettes/zucchini all over with **olive oil**. Mix **50g/1¾oz/¾ cup finely grated Parmesan cheese** with **30g/1oz/scant ⅓ cup ground almonds** in a bowl.

⊳ Dunk the courgette/zucchini sticks into the Parmesan mixture until coated, then arrange them on the baking sheets. Bake for 25–30 minutes until the coating is crisp and starting to turn golden.

(Button mushrooms and slices of aubergine/eggplant are also delicious cooked this way.)

BLACKENED CORN SALSA

A spoonful of this zingy salsa livens up veggie burgers, fritters, eggs, rice dishes and more.

⊳ Heat a griddle pan over a high heat. Brush **2 corn cobs** all over with **olive oil**, then griddle for 10 minutes, turning them every so often, or until the kernels soften and blacken in places. Slice the kernels off the cobs into a bowl and stir in **2 chopped deseeded tomatoes**, **1 diced small red pepper**, **3 finely chopped spring onions/scallions**, **1 handful of chopped coriander/cilantro leaves**, **1 tablespoon chopped jalapeño chillies** (optional). Add **a good slug of olive oil** and stir well until combined.

SUPER RED SLAW

Forget the mayonnaise-laden, shop-bought equivalent, this vibrantly coloured slaw is a real winner.

⊳ Mix together **3 handfuls of grated red cabbage**, **2 grated carrots** and **1 uncooked beetroot/beet** in a bowl. Stir in **¼ finely chopped red onion**.

⊳ Mix together **100g/3½oz/scant ½ cup plain live yogurt**, **2 tablespoons mayonnaise** and the **juice of ½ lemon**. Season the dressing with **freshly ground black pepper**. Add the yogurt dressing to the vegetables and turn until combined.

A FAMILY FAVOURITE, THESE SAUSAGES ARE A NUTRITIOUS BLEND OF CHESTNUTS, PUMPKIN SEEDS AND CHEESE. THEY'RE GOOD WITH MASHED POTATOES AND ONION GRAVY OR SERVED AS A HOTDOG IN A BUN WITH RELISH AND SALAD. IT'S WORTH MAKING DOUBLE THE QUANTITY AND THEN FREEZING THE UNCOOKED SAUSAGES – FREEZE THEM ON A BAKING SHEET, THEN TRANSFER TO A BAG WHEN FROZEN.

BANGERS *with onion gravy*

134

Serves 4
Preparation time: 20 minutes,
plus chilling
Cooking time: 25 minutes

80g/2¾oz/heaped ½ cup
    pumpkin seeds
240g/8½oz/1¾ cups cooked
    peeled chestnuts
125g/4½oz/2 cups fresh
    wholegrain breadcrumbs
1 onion, grated
1 tsp dried thyme
1 tbsp reduced-salt soy sauce
1 tbsp Dijon mustard
1 tbsp tomato purée/paste
80g/2¾oz mature/sharp
    Cheddar cheese, grated
1 egg, lightly beaten
2 tbsp sunflower oil, for frying
freshly ground black pepper
Easy Onion Gravy
    (see page 132), mashed
    potatoes and peas, to serve

1 Toast the pumpkin seeds in a large, dry frying pan for 3–4 minutes, tossing the pan occasionally, until they start to colour – take care as they can pop in the pan. Transfer to a food processor and grind to a coarse powder, then scrape them into a mixing bowl.

2 Put the chestnuts in the food processor and blitz until finely chopped, then add them to the bowl with the seeds. Stir in the remaining ingredients for the sausages until thoroughly combined and season with pepper. The mixture should hold together when pressed between your fingers.

3 Line a large baking sheet with baking parchment. Divide the chestnut mixture equally into 12, then form each portion into a sausage shape and put them on the prepared sheet. Chill in the refrigerator for 20 minutes to firm up.

4 To cook the sausages, heat half the oil in the frying pan over a medium heat. Add the sausages and cook for 6–8 minutes, turning occasionally, until golden all over. You may need to cook them in two batches, in which case add the remaining oil. (You can also bake the sausages: simply brush them lightly in oil and cook for 20 minutes in a preheated oven at 200°/400°F/Gas 6.) Serve the sausages with the onion gravy, mashed potatoes and peas.

CHESTNUTS

The fibre content of chestnuts means that this starchy food has a low glycaemic index, giving sustained amounts of energy.

I HAVEN'T MET A CHILD WHO DOESN'T LIKE NOODLES AND THE BEAUTY OF RAMEN IS ITS VERSATILITY, SO AS LONG AS THE NOODLES AND BROTH ARE AT THE HEART OF THE DISH, YOU CAN SELECT YOUR OWN FAVOURITE VEG, TOPPINGS AND OTHER ADDITIONS. THIS VERSION IS BASED ON WHAT GOES DOWN WELL IN MY HOUSE – THE PINK EGGS ARE FUN AND ADD A PROTEIN ELEMENT TO THE NOODLE BOWL.

RAMEN WITH PINK EGGS

Serves 4
Preparation time: 10 minutes, plus standing and infusing
Cooking time: 20 minutes

1.25l/44fl oz/5¼ cups reduced-salt vegetable stock

8cm/3¼in piece of fresh root ginger, peeled and sliced into rounds

3 garlic cloves, finely chopped

2 tbsp reduced-salt soy sauce

2 tsp Chinese five-spice powder

2 star anise

1 heaped tbsp dried wakame

325g/11½oz wholegrain noodles

2 carrots, cut into thin strips

4 spring onions/scallions, thinly sliced on the diagonal

1 red pepper, deseeded and cut into thin strips

200g/7oz smoked tofu/beancurd, cubed

1 tbsp black or white sesame seeds, to serve

PINK EGGS:

4 large hard-boiled eggs, peeled

2 large cooked beetroot/beets

2 tsp reduced-salt soy sauce

1 To make the pink eggs, use a stick/immersion blender to blitz the beetroot/beets to a purée. Stir in the soy sauce. Immerse the eggs in the beetroot/beet mixture and leave for at least 1 hour until they are stained pink, or leave, covered, in the refrigerator until ready to eat.

2 To make the broth, pour the vegetable stock into a large saucepan and add the ginger, garlic, soy sauce, five-spice and star anise. Stir well, bring up to the boil, then turn off the heat and leave to infuse for at least 1 hour. This stage is not essential but it adds to the flavour of the broth.

3 Soak the wakame in cold water for 5 minutes until softened, then drain (or you can use nori flakes or spinach).

4 To reheat the broth, bring it almost to the boil, then turn the heat down and simmer for 10 minutes. Remove and discard the ginger and star anise.

5 Cook the noodles in a separate pan, following the instructions on the packet, until tender. Drain the noodles, then divide among four large serving bowls. Add the wakame, carrots, the white part of the spring onions/scallions, the red pepper and tofu, then pour the broth over the top.

6 Remove the eggs from the beetroot/beet mixture (use it in the Big Veg Chilli on page 120). Halve the eggs and place on top and sprinkle with the green spring onions/scallions and seeds.

CARROTS

The potent antioxidant beta carotene, which gives carrots their vibrant orange colour, is converted to vitamin A in the body. This nutrient is vital for good vision and eye health.

HERO FOOD

I LOVE THOSE KINDS OF MEAL WHEN YOU LAY OUT ALL THE VARIOUS COMPONENTS ON THE DINING TABLE – IN THIS CASE MUSHROOM KOFTE, TACOS, CASHEW AND AVOCADO DIP, CHEESE, SALAD AND CHILLI SAUCE – AND LET EVERYONE HELP THEMSELVES. IT CERTAINLY SAVES ON SERVING TIME AND ADDS A FUN ELEMENT TO MEALTIMES.

BUILD-YOUR-OWN TACOS

Serves 4
Preparation time: 25 minutes, plus soaking
Cooking time: 25 minutes

MUSHROOM KOFTE:

2 tbsp olive oil, plus extra for brushing
300g/10½oz mushrooms, finely chopped
3 garlic cloves, finely chopped
1 tsp dried oregano
1 tbsp fajita spice mix
70g/2½oz/scant ¾ cup jumbo oats
400g/14oz can butter/lima beans, drained
1 tbsp reduced-salt soy sauce

TO SERVE:

8 corn tacos
Cashew & Avocado Dip (see page 47)
shredded crisp lettuce
grated Cheddar cheese
1 red pepper, deseeded and sliced
chilli sauce (optional)

1 Preheat the oven to 180°C/350°F/Gas 4. To make the mushroom kofte, heat the oil in a large frying pan over a medium heat. Add the mushrooms and cook for 10 minutes, turning occasionally, until there is no trace of liquid in the pan and the mushrooms start to turn golden. Add the garlic, oregano and spice mix – and a splash more oil, if needed – and cook for another minute.

2 Remove from the heat, tip half of the mushroom mixture into a food processor and the other half into a large mixing bowl and leave to cool. Add the oats, beans and soy sauce to the mushrooms in the food processor and blend to a coarse paste. You may need to scrape the mixture down the sides occasionally.

3 Scoop the bean mixture into the bowl containing the remaining mushrooms and stir until combined. Form the mixture into 16 balls about the size of a walnut.

4 Brush the balls with oil, place on a baking sheet and bake for 15 minutes, turning occasionally, until golden. Just before the kofte are ready, put the taco shells on a separate baking sheet in the oven to warm through.

5 To serve, put the kofte, tacos and dip on the table with the rest of the accompaniments and let everyone help themselves.

AVOCADO

After many years in the dark, avocados are now hailed as a 'superfood' thanks to their bountiful amount of good fats and vitamin E, which are great for the skin, hair, heart and brain.

SHOP-BOUGHT PIZZAS OFTEN FALL SHORT HEALTHWISE, BUT MAKING YOUR OWN USING A YEAST-BASED DOUGH CAN BE TIME-CONSUMING. THIS YEAST-FREE ALTERNATIVE IS QUICK AND SIMPLE, PLUS YOU CAN ADD YOUR OWN CHOICE OF HEALTHY TOPPINGS. I'VE A GIVEN A FEW SUGGESTIONS, BUT FEEL FREE TO COME UP WITH YOUR OWN.

speedy PAN PIZZAS

Makes 4
Preparation time: 20 minutes,
    plus resting
Cooking time: 30 minutes

PIZZA BASE:
400g/14oz/3¼ cups self-raising
    spelt or wheat flour, plus
    extra for dusting
1 tsp baking powder
1 tsp salt
400g/14oz/scant 1⅔ cups plain
    live yogurt
1 tsp extra virgin olive oil

TOMATO SAUCE:
250ml/9fl oz/1 cup passata
1 tbsp tomato purée/paste
1 tsp dried oregano
2 tsp extra virgin olive oil, plus
    extra for cooking and drizzling

TOPPING:
1 large handful of baby spinach
    leaves, tough stalks removed
4 eggs
175g/6oz mozzarella cheese,
    drained, patted dry and torn
    into chunks

1 To make the pizza base, mix together the flour, baking powder, salt, yogurt and oil in a large mixing bowl using a fork and then your hands until the mixture forms a soft dough. Tip the dough out onto a floured work surface and knead briefly until a smooth ball. Return the dough to the bowl, cover with cling film/plastic wrap and leave to rest for 20 minutes. (The dough can be made in advance, wrapped in cling film/plastic wrap and kept in the refrigerator for up to a day. Bring it back to room temperature before cooking.)

2 While the dough is resting, mix together the ingredients for the tomato sauce in a bowl and leave to one side.

3 Preheat the grill/broiler to high. Put the spinach in a bowl and pour over enough just-boiled water to cover. Leave for a couple of minutes until wilted, then drain and refresh under cold running water. Drain the spinach again, pat dry with paper towels and leave to one side.

4 Divide the dough into 4 pieces and roll into balls. Take one piece of the dough and roll out on a lightly floured work surface to a thin 27cm/10¾in round.

5 Heat a large, ovenproof frying pan over a medium heat and add a splash of oil to very lightly coat the bottom. Place the pizza base in the pan and press it out to the edge. Cook for 2 minutes until the base starts to turn golden underneath.

6 While the pizza is still in the pan, spread a quarter of the tomato sauce over the top of the pizza, leaving a border around the edge. Top with a quarter of the spinach, forming it into a nest with a hole in the middle. Crack an egg into the hole, then scatter over some of the mozzarella. Drizzle over a little extra olive oil.

7 Slip the pizza out of pan, place under the grill/broiler and cook for 5–8 minutes until the egg is just set.

8 While the pizza is grilling/broiling, start to prepare and cook the second pizza and repeat to make 4 in total. The pizzas are best served when freshly cooked.

➥ Pictured on page 114.

HERO FOOD

LIVE YOGURT

The gut has been called the 'second brain' and its health is vital to the wellbeing of the whole body. Live yogurt contains beneficial bacteria, which are known to support healthy digestion and benefit the gut.

MORE TOPPING IDEAS

MUSHROOM & SMOKED TOFU

8 mushrooms, thinly sliced
1 tbsp oregano
200g/7oz smoked tofu/beancurd, cut into bite-size pieces
4 tbsp mascarpone cheese

Scatter the toppings over the tomato sauce, just before grilling/broiling.

THE MEDITERRANEAN

1 roasted pepper from a jar, drained and sliced
1 small courgette/zucchini, grated
1 handful of pitted olives, sliced
175g/6oz mozzarella cheese, drained, patted dry and torn into chunks
1 handful of pine nuts
1 handful of basil leaves

Scatter the toppings over the tomato sauce, just before grilling/broiling.

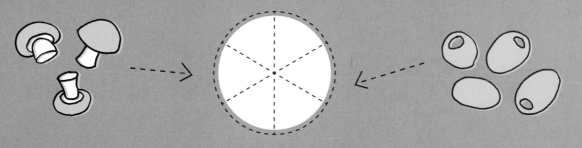

KIDS COOK SUNDAY LUNCH

NOTE TO ADULT HELPERS:

Cooking together can be a bonding time between adults and children – though I'm under no illusion that it can sometimes go the other way! I'm also a great believer that if children get involved in what's going on in the kitchen, especially helping with meal preparation, then this knowledge of cooking and ingredients will set them on the right path to being interested in food and eating well in the future. Well that's the theory . . .

Sunday is when many of us have a bit of extra time and it can be a great opportunity to get your children to do some cooking – and what could be a better meal to choose than Sunday lunch. These recipes are easy enough for a beginner cook to make with adult help, while the more accomplished will be able to make them on their own, possibly with a little adult guidance or help with the chopping and using the oven. Have fun!

TIMETABLE

1 Preheat the oven to 200°C/400°F/ Gas 6.

2 Boil the potatoes.

3 While the potatoes are boiling, make the filling for the filo parcels.

4 Drain the potatoes and prepare following the steps on page 144. Put them in the oven.

5 Assemble the filo parcels.

6 Put the filo parcels in the oven when the potatoes have been in the oven for 35 minutes.

7 Make the Leek & Cauli Cream (see page 144) and any other vegetables.

8 You're ready to serve up!

MUSHROOM FILO PARCELS

Serves 4
Preparation time: 20 minutes,
   plus cooling
Cooking time: 40 minutes

1 tbsp olive oil
1 large onion, finely chopped
300g/10½oz chestnut/cremini
   mushrooms, finely chopped
2 large garlic cloves, finely chopped
125g/4½oz/scant 1 cup cooked,
   peeled chestnuts, finely chopped
1 tsp dried thyme
80g/2¾oz sundried tomatoes in
   oil, drained, reserving 1 tbsp
   of the oil
40g/1½oz/3 tbsp butter, melted
6 sheets filo/phyllo pastry
   (270g/9½oz pack)
4 long chives (optional)

▷→ Heat the olive oil in a saucepan over a medium heat. Add the onion and cook, stirring occasionally, for 5 minutes until soft. Turn the heat down, add the mushrooms and cook for 5 minutes, stirring, until soft.

▷→ Add the garlic, chestnuts, thyme and sundried tomatoes with the reserved tomato oil and cook for 3 minutes until the filling is quite dry. Mash with a potato masher into a rough paste and leave to cool.

▷→ Preheat the oven to 200°C/400°F/Gas 6. Line a baking sheet with baking parchment.

▷→ Lay 3 of the pastry sheets out on a worktop, the long side towards you, and cut them in half vertically. Repeat with the remaining 3 pastry sheets, so you have 4 sets in total, each one made up of 3 layers.

▷→ To make a parcel, take one set (cover the rest with a damp dish towel to stop them drying out). Brush the first layer of pastry with butter and top with the second layer at an angle. Repeat with the other layer, brushing each one with butter as you go.

▷→ Place a quarter of the filling mixture in the middle of the top sheet of the filo. Draw the edges of the pastry up around the filling and press them together at the top to seal into a money-bag shape.

▷→ Place the parcel on the prepared baking sheet and repeat to make 4 parcels in total. Brush the parcels with any remaining butter and bake for 20–25 minutes until golden and crisp all over. Just before serving, you could tie a chive around the neck of each parcel like a ribbon, if you like.

CRISPY ROASTIES

Serves 4
Preparation time: 5 minutes
Cooking time: 70 minutes

about 12–16 even-size waxy
  potatoes, such as Charlotte,
  washed and patted dry
1 tbsp olive oil
30g/1oz/2 tbsp butter

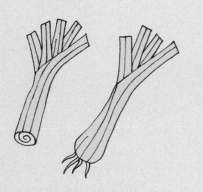

⊐⇒ Preheat the oven to 200°C/400°F/Gas 6.

⊐⇒ Cook the potatoes in a pan of boiling water
for 5–8 minutes until they start to soften but aren't
completely cooked. Carefully drain the potatoes and
return them to the pan to dry in the heat of the turned-
off hob/stovetop. Add the oil and turn the potatoes
with a large spoon until they are coated in the oil.

⊐⇒ Arrange the potatoes in an even layer on a large
baking sheet. Using a potato masher, lightly crush
the top of each potato – you just want the tops to crack
slightly, but not the whole potato to fall apart.

⊐⇒ Place a knob of butter on top of each potato and
roast in the oven for about 1 hour, or until the skins
are crisp and golden and the insides tender.

LEEK & CAULI CREAM

Serves 4
Preparation time: 5 minutes
Cooking time: 10 minutes

2 leeks, sliced
1 cauliflower, broken into florets
100ml/3½fl oz/scant ½ cup hot
  reduced-salt vegetable stock
3 tbsp crème fraîche or cream

⊐⇒ Put the leeks and cauliflower in the basket of a
steamer pan over gently boiling water. Cover with a lid
and cook for 5 minutes, or until tender.

⊐⇒ Transfer the steamed vegetables to a saucepan
and add the vegetable stock and crème fraîche, heat
through, then use a stick/immersion blender to purée
until smooth and creamy. Add more stock or crème
fraîche, if needed.

You're now ready to serve up Sunday lunch!

DESSERTS
& TREATS

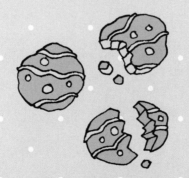

← LEFT, COCONUT-BANANA ICE. RECIPE ON PAGE 159.

CREAMY, RICH AND CHOCOLATEY – THIS IS EVERYTHING A
CHOCOLATE MOUSSE SHOULD BE AND NO ONE WILL KNOW
THAT IT CONTAINS AVOCADO. BEST KEEP IT A SECRET!

STRAWBERRY CHOC POTS

Serves 4
**Preparation time: 10 minutes,
plus soaking and chilling**

70g/2½oz/½ cup soft, pitted
dried dates, roughly chopped

1 large, ripe avocado, pitted and
flesh scooped out

30g/1oz/scant ⅓ cup good-
quality unsweetened cocoa
powder or raw cacao

1 tsp coconut oil, melted

1 tsp vanilla extract

4 tsp maple syrup or clear honey

100ml/3½fl oz/scant ½ cup
coconut drinking milk

strawberries, hulled and halved
or quartered, to serve

1 Put the dates in a bowl and cover with 80ml/2½fl oz/⅓ cup
just-boiled water. Leave the dates to soften for 30 minutes.

2 Put the dates and soaking water in a blender or food
processor with the avocado, unsweetened cocoa powder,
coconut oil, vanilla, maple syrup and milk and blend until
smooth and creamy.

3 Spoon the mixture into small glasses, cups or ramekins/
custard cups and chill for 20 minutes to firm up a little.
Serve topped with strawberries.

COCOA
Rich in antioxidants, including
flavonoids, good-quality unsweetened
cocoa (or preferably the unrefined
raw cacao) is believed to benefit the
health of the heart as well as make
us feel good!

MY FAVOURITE DESSERTS TEND TO BE THOSE THAT DON´T TAKE TOO LONG TO MAKE . . . TIME JUST DOESN´T ALLOW FOR FANCY PUDDINGS. THIS CREAMY, LIGHT, FRUITY DESSERT TICKS ALL THE RIGHT BOXES. BE AWARE THAT IT CONTAINS RAW EGG WHITES.

RASPBERRY YOGURT MOUSSE

Serves 4
Preparation time: 15 minutes,
plus chilling

300g/10½oz/1¼ cups thick plain live yogurt
2–3 tbsp maple syrup or clear honey
1 tsp vanilla extract
4 handfuls of raspberries
2 egg whites

1 Mix together the yogurt, maple syrup and vanilla in a large mixing bowl until combined.

2 Crush half the raspberries with the back of a fork, then stir them into the yogurt mixture. Taste for sweetness, adding a little more syrup, if needed, then leave to one side.

3 In a large, clean, grease-free bowl, whisk the eggs whites to stiff peaks. Using a metal spoon, fold a large spoonful of the egg whites into the yogurt mixture, then fold in the remaining egg whites, taking care to retain as much of the air as possible.

4 Spoon the mixture into four small tumblers, then chill for 30 minutes, or until slightly firm. If in a hurry, don´t worry about chilling – just eat straightaway. Scatter over the remaining raspberries and serve.

RASPBERRIES
Brimming with vitamin C, this nutrient is a potent antioxidant that helps to boost the immune system. Eating raspberries is also said to improve vision and eye health due to the presence of ellagic acid.

SIMPLY DELICIOUS – GRATED APPLES (STILL WITH THEIR
NUTRITIOUS SKINS) ARE COOKED UNTIL SOFT AND MUSHY AND
SERVED TOPPED WITH SWEET AND CRISP TOASTED CINNAMON
CRUMBS. I LIKE A SPOONFUL OF CASHEW CREAM, TOO, BUT YOU
COULD USE REGULAR CREAM OR THICK LIVE YOGURT.

APPLE MUSH
with cinnamon crumbs

Serves 4
Preparation time: 5 minutes
Cooking time: 5 minutes

4 dessert apples, with skins,
    cored and grated
good squeeze of lemon juice
4–6 tbsp fresh apple juice
1 large handful of raisins
    (optional)
Cashew Cream (see page 163)
    or thick live yogurt
Crunchy Cinnamon Crumbs
    (see page 163)

1 To make the apple mush, put the apples in a pan with
the lemon juice (to stop them browning), apple juice and
raisins, if using. Cook over a medium-low heat, part-covered
with a lid and stirring occasionally, for 5 minutes until soft
and mushy. Towards the end of the cooking time, crush the
apples with the back of a spoon to help the fruit break down.

2 Spoon the apples into a bowl and top with a spoonful
of the cashew cream or yogurt, then sprinkle some of the
crunchy cinnamon crumbs over the top.

HERO FOOD

RAISINS
Like other dried fruit, raisins are a good
source of fibre and a concentrated source
of energy, vitamins and minerals.

THE ADDITION OF THE DELICATELY FLAVOURED RICOTTA ADDS A
WELCOME PROTEIN BOOST TO THESE PANCAKES, WHILE THE BANANA
LENDS NATURAL SWEETNESS. THEY COME WITH ROASTED PINEAPPLE
AND A COCONUT VANILLA CREAM – A PERFECT COMBINATION!

RICOTTA HOTCAKES
with roasted pineapple

Serves 4
Preparation time: 15 minutes,
plus resting and chilling
Cooking time: 20 minutes

100g/3½oz/heaped ¾ cup spelt
 or plain/all-purpose flour
1 tsp baking powder
2 eggs, lightly beaten
100ml/3½fl oz/scant ½ cup
 almond milk or milk of choice
½ tsp vanilla extract
125g/4½oz/scant ⅔ cup ricotta
 cheese, drained
2 bananas, mashed
½ tsp ground cinnamon, to serve

ROASTED PINEAPPLE:

1 tbsp coconut oil, plus extra
 for cooking the hotcakes
½ small ripe pineapple, skin
 and central core removed,
 cut into large bite-size chunks

COCONUT VANILLA CREAM:

100ml/3½fl oz/scant ½ cup thick
 coconut cream from the top
 of a can of coconut milk
1 tsp vanilla extract
1–2 tbsp maple syrup or honey

1 To make the hotcakes, sift the flour and baking powder into
a mixing bowl. Mix together the eggs, milk, vanilla and ricotta
until combined, then beat into the flour mixture to make a
smooth batter. Leave to rest for 20 minutes and chill the can
of coconut milk at the same time to make it easier to separate.

2 To make the coconut vanilla cream, spoon the thick coconut
cream from the top of the can of coconut milk into a bowl
(leaving the watery residue). Add the rest of the ingredients
and beat together until smooth and creamy. Leave to one side.

3 To roast the pineapple, heat the coconut oil in a large frying
pan over a medium heat. Add the pineapple and cook for a few
minutes until tender and starting to colour. Transfer to a bowl,
cover with foil and keep warm in a low oven.

4 Heat enough of the coconut oil to lightly coat the bottom of
the frying pan. Place three or four 50ml/1¾fl oz/scant ¼ cup
spoonfuls of the batter in the pan and cook for 2–3 minutes on
each side until golden. Keep them warm in the oven while you
make the remaining pancakes – about 12 in total.

5 Serve the pancakes with the pineapple and the coconut
vanilla cream, sprinkled with cinnamon.

THESE MINI CHEESECAKES ARE JUST THE RIGHT SIZE FOR KIDS AND ARE GIVEN A NUTRITIONAL BOOST WITH A BASE MADE OF NUTS AND SEEDS RATHER THAN THE MORE USUAL SUGARY BISCUITS. LIKEWISE, THE FILLING IS GIVEN EXTRA OOMPH WITH THE HELP OF THE SESAME SEED PASTE, TAHINI. I'VE GONE FOR A TOPPING OF FRESH, RIPE MANGO, BUT DO TRY OTHER FAVOURITE FRUITS.

MANGO CHEESECAKES

Makes 4
Preparation time: 15 minutes,
plus chilling
Cooking time: 4 minutes

1 large ripe mango, pitted, peeled and diced, to serve

FILLING:
150g/5½oz cream cheese
4 tsp tahini paste
1 tsp vanilla extract
4 tsp maple syrup or clear honey

NUT & DATE BASE:
60g/2¼oz/scant ⅔ cup pecan nuts
30g/1oz/¼ cup sunflower seeds
4 soft, pitted dried dates, chopped
1 heaped tbsp smooth peanut butter
1 heaped tsp coconut oil
1 tbsp maple syrup or honey

1 To make the base, put the pecans and sunflower seeds in a large, dry frying pan and toast over a medium-low heat for 4 minutes, turning once, until they smell slightly toasted. Leave to cool. Transfer to a mini food processor with the rest of the ingredients for the base. Process until finely chopped, then spoon into four small glasses or large ramekins/custard cups and press down with the back of a spoon.

2 To make the filling, put all the ingredients in a blender and blend to a smooth cream. Spoon the mixture into the glasses or ramekins/custard cups and smooth the tops. Chill for 30 minutes until slightly firm – if you can wait.

3 Just before serving, scatter the diced mango over the top of each cheesecake.

HERO FOOD

MANGOES
Rich in vitamin C and beta carotene, mango is a natural prebiotic and helps with digestion.

I LIKE TO MAKE INDIVIDUAL-SIZE DESSERTS – NOT ONLY DO THEY LOOK CUTE BUT YOU ARE ALSO SURREPTITIOUSLY CONTROLLING PORTION SIZE. YOU COULD MAKE A LARGE BATCH OF THE CRUMBLE TOPPING AND STORE IT IN A BAG IN THE FREEZER FOR NEXT TIME.

RHUBARB AND RASPBERRY CRUMBLES

Serves 4
Preparation time: 15 minutes
Cooking time: 40 minutes

200g/7oz rhubarb, cut into 2.5cm/1in pieces

2 tbsp light soft brown sugar

juice and finely grated zest of ½ orange

4 handfuls of raspberries

Vanilla Custard (see page 163), cream or ice cream, to serve

CRUMBLE TOPPING:

30g/1oz/⅓ cup buckwheat flakes or quinoa flakes

50g/1¾oz/scant ½ cup wholegrain spelt or plain/all-purpose flour

30g/1oz/2 tbsp chilled butter, cubed

30g/1oz/⅓ cup pecan nuts, roughly chopped

1 tbsp light soft brown sugar

1 Preheat the oven to 190°C/375°F/Gas 5.

2 Put the rhubarb, sugar and orange juice in a saucepan and bring almost to the boil, then turn the heat down and simmer, part-covered with a lid, for 5 minutes until tender but not mushy. Stir in the orange zest and the raspberries and transfer the fruity mixture to four deep ramekins/custard cups or small ovenproof bowls.

3 While the rhubarb is cooking, put the buckwheat flakes and flour in a mixing bowl. Using your fingertips, lightly rub the butter into the flour mixture until it resembles coarse breadcrumbs. Stir in the pecans and brown sugar.

4 Sprinkle the crumble mixture over the top of the fruit in an even layer. Put the ramekins/custard cups in a baking pan in the oven for 30–35 minutes, or until the crumble topping has turned crisp and light golden. Leave to cool slightly before serving with custard, cream or ice cream.

RHUBARB
Rhubarb is a good source of vitamin K – this nutrient supports healthy bones.

PERFECT FOR BREAKFAST OR AS A DESSERT, THIS CREAMY
STRAWBERRY CONFECTION USES TOASTED BUCKWHEAT, ALSO
KNOWN AS KASHA. THE GRAIN HAS A NUTTY FLAVOUR – MAKE SURE
YOU USE THE TOASTED VARIETY – AND IS SOAKED, RATHER THAN
COOKED, SO THIS DESSERT NEEDS A BIT OF FORWARD PLANNING.

STRAWBERRY *swirls*

Serves 4
Preparation: 10 minutes,
plus soaking and freezing

50g/1¾oz/⅓ cup toasted
buckwheat groats (kasha)

2 large bananas, thickly sliced

400g/14oz/4 cups strawberries,
hulled

1 tbsp ground linseeds/
flaxseeds

1 tsp vanilla extract

1 tsp ground cinnamon

2–3 tbsp maple syrup or clear
honey

4 tbsp milk of choice, or enough
to loosen

1 Put the buckwheat in a bowl, cover with just-boiled water
and leave to soak, covered, for 8 hours or overnight. Drain
the buckwheat and rinse under cold running water to remove
any stickiness. Leave to drain in the sieve/fine-mesh strainer.

2 While the buckwheat is soaking, put the bananas in a
freezer bag and freeze for 3 hours, or overnight, until frozen.

3 Blend the strawberries until puréed, then set aside one-
third in a bowl, leaving the remaining purée in the blender.

4 Add the buckwheat, bananas, linseeds/flaxseeds, vanilla,
cinnamon, maple syrup and milk to the blender and blend
to a thick, creamy consistency. Check for sweetness and add
more syrup, if needed, or, if too thick, add a splash more milk.

5 Spoon the mixture into glasses and swirl in the reserved
strawberry purée. Chill until ready to serve.

TOASTED BUCKWHEAT (KASHA)

High in iron, magnesium and zinc,
gluten-free buckwheat is said to benefit
the health of the heart.

FROZEN BANANAS MAKE THE EASIEST ICE CREAM EVER. SIMPLY BLEND THEM WITH COCONUT CREAM AND CRÈME FRAÎCHE UNTIL SMOOTH AND CREAMY – JOB DONE! FOR A DAIRY-FREE VERSION JUST USE THE COCONUT. THE EASIEST WAY TO SEPARATE THE CREAM IN A CAN OF COCONUT MILK IS TO PUT THE CAN IN THE REFRIGERATOR FOR 1 HOUR – THE CREAM SHOULD RISE TO THE TOP, READY TO BE SCOOPED OFF.

COCONUT-BANANA ICE

Serves 4
Preparation time: 10 minutes,
plus freezing

4 bananas, peeled and cut into chunks

2 tbsp desiccated/dried shredded coconut, plus extra for sprinkling

5 tbsp thick coconut cream from the top of a can of coconut milk

5 tbsp crème fraîche

2 tbsp maple syrup or clear honey, or to taste

fresh fruit (optional), to serve

1 Put the bananas in a freezer bag and freeze for 3 hours until frozen.

2 While the bananas are freezing, toast the coconut in a large, dry frying pan over a medium-low heat for 3 minutes, shaking the pan occasionally, until slightly golden. Tip into a bowl and leave to cool.

3 When the bananas are frozen, put them in a blender and blitz until almost smooth. Add the coconut cream, crème fraîche and maple syrup and blitz again until smooth. Taste and add more sweetener, if needed. If the banana ice is soft, return it to the freezer to firm up. Serve it in scoops, sprinkled with coconut and fresh fruit, if you like.

⇨ Pictured on page 146.

HERO FOOD

BANANAS

Bananas are rich in the mineral potassium, which is important for the functioning of cells, nerves and muscles.

CHERRY POPSICLES

Makes 6–8
Preparation time: 10 minutes,
plus freezing

300g/10½oz/1⅔ cups frozen
   pitted dark cherries

2 ripe nectarines, halved, pitted
   and chopped

2 tbsp maple syrup or clear
   honey, or to taste

½ recipe quantity cold Vanilla
   Custard (see page 163) or
   175ml/6fl oz/¾ cup ready-
   made fresh custard

1 Put the cherries, nectarines, maple syrup and custard in
a blender and blend until smooth and creamy. If the motor of
your blender isn't up to it, you may have to semi-defrost the
cherries first. Taste and check the sweetness, adding a splash
more syrup, if needed.

2 Spoon the fruit mixture into six to eight lolly moulds,
depending on their size, and freeze until firm.

3 To serve, take the popsicles out of the freezer and leave
to soften slightly before removing them from the moulds.

DARK CHERRIES

Dark-coloured cherries have a higher
level of potent antioxidants than light
ones. They are also a good source of
vitamins A and C as well as iron. What's
more, they are reputed to help you sleep.

QUICK IDEAS

FUSS-FREE DESSERTS

ON A DAY-TO-DAY BASIS, I'M NOT A GREAT ONE FOR MAKING DESSERTS, BUT AN OCCASIONAL SWEET SOMETHING ALWAYS GOES DOWN A TREAT – AS LONG AS IT'S SIMPLE, QUICK AND NOT TOO SUGARY.

MORE OFTEN THAN NOT, IT'S A HOMEMADE DAIRY-FREE CASHEW CREAM, VANILLA CUSTARD OR CRUNCHY CINNAMON CRUMBS SPOONED OVER FRESH OR COOKED FRUIT, THICK PLAIN YOGURT OR ICE CREAM – JUST ENOUGH TO ADD A BIT OF OOMPH. ANOTHER FAVOURITE IS THESE BITE-SIZE, YOGURT-COVERED FROZEN FRUITY TREATS – SIMPLE.

RECIPES SERVE 4.

YO-FRO FRUITY POPS

A simple treat to keep in the freezer.

▷→ To make the yogurt-coated fruit pops, mix together **100g/3½oz/scant ½ cup thick Greek yogurt** or **coconut yogurt**, **1 teaspoon vanilla extract** and **2 teaspoons maple syrup** or **clear honey** in a bowl until combined. You're now ready to start dunking (see below) . . .

▷→ For banana pops, slice **1 large, peeled banana** into three chunks and insert a lolly/popsicle stick into the base of each one. Holding the stick, dunk the banana pops into the yogurt mixture until coated. Place, stick pointing upwards, on a baking-parchment-lined baking sheet and put them in the freezer for a few hours until frozen.

▷→ To make strawberry pops, hold onto the stalk of a **large strawberry** and dunk it into the yogurt mixture until three-quarters coated, then place on a baking-parchment-lined baking sheet. Repeat until you have about 16 yogurt-coated strawberries and freeze until frozen.

▷→ For blueberry bites, dunk **a couple of handfuls of blueberries** into the bowl of yogurt mixture until they are completely coated. Using a teaspoon, fish out the berries and place them on a baking-parchment-lined baking sheet in the freezer until frozen.

When the yo-fro fruity pops are frozen, transfer them to a freezer-proof bag. They can be kept in the freezer until ready to eat and any leftover yogurt can be blobbed directly onto a lined baking sheet in small peaked rounds, then frozen until solid. Decant the yogurt blobs to a freezer-proof bag. You'll need to let the fruit soften slightly before eating.

CRUNCHY CINNAMON CRUMBS

A sprinkling of these golden, nutty crumbs can turn a simple bowl of cooked fruit or yogurt into something a bit more special. They will keep in an airtight container in the refrigerator for up to 2 weeks.

▷ Melt **40g/1½oz/3 tbsp butter** in a large frying pan over a medium-low heat. Add **60g/2¼oz/1 cup day-old fresh wholegrain breadcrumbs**, **30g/1oz/heaped ¼ cup chopped walnuts** or **almonds** and **1 heaped tablespoon sunflower seeds**. Toast, stirring regularly to stop them burning, for about 3 minutes until golden and starting to turn crisp. Stir in **1 teaspoon ground cinnamon** and **2 teaspoons light soft brown sugar**, then remove from the heat and tip into a bowl. Leave to cool before serving.

COCONUT SPRINKLE

Use this tasty sprinkle in the same way as the Crunchy Cinnamon Crumbs, above.

▷ Toast **1 large handful of desiccated/dried shredded coconut** in a large, dry frying pan until starting to turn golden, then tip the coconut into a bowl. Toast **2 tablespoons sesame seeds** in the pan until pale golden. Add to the bowl and leave to cool.

CASHEW CREAM

A bowl of this thick, surprisingly creamy dairy-free cream goes with fruit, cakes, pies and other lovely things.

▷ Put **70g/2½oz/scant ½ cup cashew nuts** in a bowl and cover with just-boiled water. Leave to soak for 1 hour until softened. Drain the nuts, discarding the soaking water, and tip them into a food processor or blender with **6 tablespoons milk of choice**, **1 teaspoon vanilla extract** and **1 tablespoon maple syrup** or **clear honey**. Blend, occasionally scraping the mixture down the sides of the bowl, until smooth and creamy – add a splash more milk, if too thick. Spoon into a bowl, cover with cling film/plastic wrap and chill until needed.

VANILLA CUSTARD

Custard with fruit, custard mixed into live yogurt, custard poured over sweet pies and tarts, frozen custard popsicles and my go-to pud, bananas and custard – you name it, there's lots you can do with a pot of custard.

▷ Warm **300ml/10½fl oz/scant 1¼ cups milk** and **1 teaspoon vanilla extract** in a saucepan. Meanwhile, whisk together **2 large egg yolks**, **2–3 tablespoons honey** or **maple syrup** and **1 heaped teaspoon cornflour/cornstarch** in a large heatproof bowl. Pour the warmed milk gradually into the egg mixture, whisking continuously. Return the custard to the pan and heat gently over a very low heat, stirring with a wooden spoon until thickened.

REMINISCENT OF THAT WELL-KNOWN CHOCOLATE PEANUT CONFECTIONERY, THIS VERSION MAKES A PERFECT SNACK OR FUSS-FREE DESSERT. YOU COULD SWAP THE CHOICE OF NUTS OR SEEDS – JUST KEEP THE RATIOS THE SAME. THE PLAIN AND WHITE CHOCOLATE SWIRLY-PATTERNED TOPPING ADDS THE FINISHING TOUCH.

PUFFED RICE BARS

Makes 16
Preparation time: 15 minutes,
**   plus chilling**
Cooking time: 10 minutes

3 tbsp coconut oil

125g/4½oz/scant 1 cup soft, pitted dried dates, finely chopped

2 tbsp maple syrup or clear honey

juice of ½ orange

300g/10½oz/1⅓ cups no-added sugar smooth peanut butter

50g/1¾oz/heaped ⅓ cup hazelnuts, roughly chopped

2 tbsp sunflower seeds

1 tbsp hemp seeds

50g/1¾oz/1¾ cups wholegrain, sugar-free puffed rice

125g/4½oz plain/semisweet chocolate, broken into squares

50g/1¾oz white chocolate, broken into squares

1 Line a 28 x 20cm/11¼ x 8in baking pan with cling film/plastic wrap and leave to one side. Put the coconut oil, dates, maple syrup, orange juice and peanut butter in a small saucepan and warm over a medium-low heat for 3–4 minutes, stirring often, until the dates break down – mash them with the back of a fork to help.

2 Meanwhile, put the hazelnuts, seeds and puffed rice in a bowl and mix together until combined.

3 Pour the peanut butter mixture into the bowl and turn gently until everything is mixed together. Spoon the mixture into the prepared pan, spread it out into an even layer using the back of a spoon (it helps if you dampen the spoon). Set aside.

4 Melt the plain/semisweet chocolate in a heatproof bowl set over a pan of gently simmering water, making sure the base does not touch the water. Spoon the melted chocolate over the peanut butter mixture, spreading it out in an even layer.

5 Melt the white chocolate, taking care not to overheat it. Dollop blobs of the melted white chocolate over the plain/semisweet chocolate, then use a skewer to swirl the chocolate and make a patterned top. Chill for 1 hour or so until firm, then serve cut into squares. Store, covered with cling film/plastic wrap, in the refrigerator – it will happily keep for 2 weeks, if it lasts that long.

THIS CAKE IS SWEETENED WITH A MIXTURE OF MINERAL-RICH BANANAS AND DARK, STICKY MOLASSES. I WASN'T QUITE SURE THE CAKE WAS GOING TO WORK BUT THE RICH, MOIST SPONGE COMBINED WITH THE CINNAMON CREAM CHEESE FROSTING WENT DOWN REALLY WELL.

BANANA <u>AND</u> GINGER CAKE

166

Makes about 12 slices
Preparation time: 20 minutes, plus cooling
Cooking time: 50 minutes

125ml/4fl oz/½ cup melted coconut oil or sunflower oil, plus extra for greasing
200g/7oz/scant 1¾ cups spelt or plain/all-purpose flour
1 tsp baking powder
pinch of sea salt
1 tbsp ground ginger
1 tsp ground cinnamon
200ml/7fl oz/scant 1 cup blackstrap molasses
3 eggs
3 bananas, mashed

CINNAMON FROSTING:
185g/6½oz cream cheese
2–3 tbsp honey, or to taste
2 tsp vanilla extract
1½ tsp ground cinnamon

1 Preheat the oven to 180°C/350°F/Gas 4. Lightly grease a 450g/1lb loaf pan.

2 Sift together the flour, baking powder, salt and spices into a large mixing bowl, then stir until combined.

3 Beat together the oil, molasses and eggs until combined, then stir in the bananas. Pour the mixture into the dry ingredients and beat together until combined. Transfer the cake mixture to the prepared loaf pan and bake for 45–50 minutes, or until a skewer inserted in the middle comes out clean.

4 While the cake is baking, make the cinnamon frosting. Put all the ingredients in a bowl and beat together until smooth, thick and creamy, then chill to firm up until ready to use.

5 Leave the cake to cool for a couple of minutes in the pan, then turn it out onto a wire rack to cool completely. When cool, spread the cinnamon frosting over the top of the cake before serving in slices.

BLACKSTRAP MOLASSES
Unlike refined white sugar, blackstrap molasses contains useful amounts of minerals such as iron, magnesium, calcium, potassium and selenium.

KIDS COOK — SWEET CHOCCY GIFTS

NOTE TO ADULT HELPERS:

We all need to be mindful of the amount of sugar or sweet things in our diets. But I'm a great one for everything in moderation and the occasional sweet treat is one of life's pleasures.

Making cakes and cookies is a great introduction to cooking for many kids. It's a good way to show them the workings of the hob/stovetop or oven, the various tools in the kitchen and different ingredients.

These recipes are the perfect starting point for the beginner cook (don't let that put you off if you're a good cook as they are all delicious) and they make great gifts wrapped up in a cellophane bag or pretty box. The sugar content has deliberately been kept as low as feasible without spoiling their taste or texture.

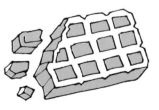

CHOCOLATE BEAN BROWNIES

Makes 12
Preparation time: 15 minutes
Cooking time: 25 minutes

80ml/2½fl oz/⅓ cup melted coconut oil or sunflower oil, plus extra for greasing
100g/3½oz/heaped ¾ cup spelt or plain/all-purpose flour
2 tsp baking powder
50g/1¾oz/½ cup unsweetened cocoa powder or raw cacao
175g/6oz/scant 1 cup light soft brown sugar
pinch of sea salt
400g/14oz can borlotti beans, drained and rinsed
3 large eggs, light beaten
1 tsp vanilla extract
2 tbsp milk of choice

⊏→ Preheat the oven to 180°C/350°F/Gas 4. Line the base and grease the sides of a 20cm/8in brownie pan.

⊏→ Sift the flour, baking powder, unsweetened cocoa powder, sugar and salt into the bowl of a food processor.

Add the rest of the ingredients and blend to a smooth batter, occasionally stopping to scrape the mixture down the sides.

➡ Spoon the cake batter into the prepared pan and spread out evenly. Bake for 20–25 minutes until risen and just cooked through – you want it to be a little squidgy in the middle. Leave to cool for a couple of minutes in the pan, then turn the cake out onto a wire rack to cool completely. Cut into 12 squares.

CHOCCY-NUT BALLS

Makes 24
Preparation time: 20 minutes,
    plus soaking and chilling
Cooking time: 4 minutes

150g/5½oz/heaped 1 cup soft, pitted
    dried dates, chopped
juice and finely grated zest of 1 orange
100g/3½oz/heaped ¾ cup cashew nuts
50g/1¾oz/heaped ⅓ cup hazelnuts
1 tbsp hemp seeds
5 tbsp unsweetened cocoa powder or
    raw cacao, plus extra for coating
6 tbsp desiccated/dried shredded
    coconut, for coating

⊃➔ Put the dates and orange juice in a bowl to soak.

⊃➔ Toast the cashews and hazelnuts in a large, dry frying pan over a medium-low heat for 4 minutes, shaking the pan until they start to colour. Tip into a food processor and blitz until finely chopped. Put the nuts in a large mixing bowl.

⊃➔ Add the soaked dates with the orange juice to the processor and blend to an almost smooth purée, pushing the dates down the sides of the processor.

⊃➔ Spoon the date mixture into the bowl containing the nuts. Stir in the hemp seeds and unsweetened cocoa powder until mixed to a thick paste.

⊃➔ Cover a small plate with a layer of unsweetened cocoa powder and a second plate with the coconut.

⊃➔ Divide the mixture in half, then divide one half evenly into 12 pieces. Roll each one into a ball, about the size of a large marble, then roll them in the cocoa powder until evenly coated.

⊃➔ Repeat with the remaining half of the date mixture, this time dunking the balls into the coconut to make about 12 balls in total. Arrange all the balls on a plate and chill for 1 hour to firm up. Store in an airtight container in the refrigerator.

PEANUT CHOCOLATE-DRIZZLE COOKIES

Makes: 12
Preparation time: 15 minutes,
plus cooling and setting
Cooking time: 25 minutes

50g/1¾oz/3½ tbsp coconut oil,
melted
90g/3¼oz/½ cup light soft
brown sugar
100g/3½oz/scant ½ cup
no-added sugar crunchy
peanut butter
1 egg, lightly beaten
100g/3½oz/⅔ cup wholegrain
spelt flour or plain/
all-purpose flour
½ tsp baking powder
½ tsp bicarbonate of soda/
baking soda
40g/1½oz plain/semisweet
or milk chocolate, broken
into small pieces

⇨ Preheat the oven to 180°C/350°F/Gas 4.
Line a baking sheet with baking parchment.

⇨ Pour the melted coconut oil into a large
mixing bowl. Using a wooden spoon, stir in
the sugar and peanut butter until combined.
Next, stir in the egg until mixed in.

⇨ Mix together the flour, baking powder and
bicarbonate of soda/baking soda. Gently fold the
flour mixture into the peanut butter mixture in
two halves until well blended.

⇨ Place large heaped dessertspoons of the
cookie mixture onto the prepared baking sheet.
Bake for 15–18 minutes until cooked but still
a little soft in the middle.

⇨ Leave the cookies to cool for a couple of
minutes, then use a spatula to move them to
a wire rack to cool completely.

⇨ Melt the chocolate in a heatproof bowl set
over a pan of gently simmering water, making
sure the base of the bowl does not touch the
water. Using oven gloves, carefully remove
the bowl from the pan.

⇨ Using a teaspoon, drizzle the chocolate
over the top of the cooled cookies. Leave the
chocolate to set and harden.

INDEX

Big thanks go to the fabulous team at Watkins for their ongoing support
over the many years that we have worked together. To Grace Cheetham for
commissioning me as well as her unfailing enthusiasm; to the multi-talented
Rebecca Woods for her editorial support and food styling; to designers
Viki Ottewill and Allan Sommerville for their creativity and patience; to
photographer Tony Briscoe and prop stylist Lucy Harvey; and last but not least
to editor Wendy Hobson for just being so good and always professional.

Finally to my lovely family for letting me test the recipes on you and for your
enthusiastic (well most of the time) feedback – Silvio, Ella and Joel. x

NOURISH
EAT WELL, LIVE WELL